Apress Pocket Guides

Apress Pocket Guides present concise summaries of cutting-edge developments and working practices throughout the tech industry. Shorter in length, books in this series aim to deliver quick-to-read guides that are easy to absorb, perfect for the time-poor professional.

This series covers the full spectrum of topics relevant to the modern industry, from security, AI, machine learning, cloud computing, web development, product design, to programming techniques and business topics too.

Typical topics might include:

- A concise guide to a particular topic, method, function or framework

- Professional best practices and industry trends

- A snapshot of a hot or emerging topic

- Industry case studies

- Concise presentations of core concepts suited for students and those interested in entering the tech industry

- Short reference guides outlining 'need-to-know' concepts and practices.

More information about this series at `https://link.springer.com/bookseries/17385`.

CI/CD Unleashed

Turbocharging Software Deployment for Quicker Delivery

Tommy Clark

Apress®

CI/CD Unleashed: Turbocharging Software Deployment for Quicker Delivery

Tommy Clark
Manchester, UK

ISBN-13 (pbk): 979-8-8688-1208-8   ISBN-13 (electronic): 979-8-8688-1209-5
https://doi.org/10.1007/979-8-8688-1209-5

Managing Director, Apress Media LLC: Welmoed Spahr
Acquisitions Editor: James Robinson-Prior
Development Editor: James Markham
Editorial Assistant: Gryffin Winkler

Cover designed by eStudioCalamar

Distributed to the book trade worldwide by Springer Science+Business Media New York, 1 New York Plaza, Suite 4600, New York, NY 10004-1562, USA. Phone 1-800-SPRINGER, fax (201) 348-4505, e-mail orders-ny@springer-sbm.com, or visit www.springeronline.com. Apress Media, LLC is a California LLC and the sole member (owner) is Springer Science + Business Media Finance Inc (SSBM Finance Inc). SSBM Finance Inc is a **Delaware** corporation.

For information on translations, please e-mail booktranslations@springernature.com; for reprint, paperback, or audio rights, please e-mail bookpermissions@springernature.com.

Apress titles may be purchased in bulk for academic, corporate, or promotional use. eBook versions and licenses are also available for most titles. For more information, reference our Print and eBook Bulk Sales web page at http://www.apress.com/bulk-sales.

Any source code or other supplementary material referenced by the author in this book is available to readers on GitHub. For more detailed information, please visit https://www.apress.com/gp/services/source-code.

If disposing of this product, please recycle the paper

Table of Contents

About the Author

 **Tommy Clark** has over ten years of experience in software development as a principal developer, solutions designer, and technical team lead. He has worked in industries as diverse as music, oil, e-commerce, and the charity sector, for organizations like Sainsbury's, Deloitte, and Cancer Research UK. Tommy's career so far has been dedicated to the transformative impact of working smarter and faster. Currently serving as a principal engineer at MoneySupermarket Group, he is passionate about championing improvements to CI/CD processes both within the company and in the broader tech community, including sharing his knowledge at local tech conferences.

About the Technical Reviewer

Owen Parker is a technical leader with ten years of experience across a range of industries including finance and semiconductor organizations. Owen has recently taken on a fresh challenge, joining MICHELIN Connected Fleet as their first dedicated release manager in order to drive forward improvements to the release process for a complex, multi-platform SaaS product. Owen has previously led high-performing DevOps teams, with a particular focus on driving value and benefit from a range of business-facing systems.

CHAPTER 1

Introduction to Continuous Integration and Continuous Deployment

Software is at the absolute core of almost every successful business I've worked in. It is vital to almost every organization in almost every industry.

In the retail industry, technology allows organizations to streamline their operations, utilize more efficient inventory management techniques, and ensure products are readily available where and when they are needed. Advanced analytics predict customer trends, improving stock levels and reducing waste, while automated systems handle restocking and order fulfilment.

In music, digital platforms have revolutionized distribution, enabling artists to reach global audiences at the click of their fingers. Sophisticated royalty tracking and payment mechanisms have allowed artists to benefit from that new global reach, while advanced data analytics aid

© Tommy Clark 2025
T. Clark, *CI/CD Unleashed*, Apress Pocket Guides,
https://doi.org/10.1007/979-8-8688-1209-5_1

both creators and music platforms in understanding their audience demographics and engagement patterns, allowing them to tailor their art to maximize both impact and revenue.

In the oil industry, geoprediction software has increased efficiency and effectiveness in oil and gas extraction processes, reducing environmental impact and costs. These advanced systems not only aid in locating oil and gas reserves but also advise on extraction methods, ensuring minimal waste and maximum yield. Predictive maintenance technologies have prevented equipment failures and downtime, further enhancing operational efficiency and environmental safety.

The charity sector has embraced digital platforms to engage supporters, facilitating global fundraising efforts to combat deadly diseases or homelessness, streamlining operations to focus on the most important or affected areas more swiftly. These platforms leverage modern techniques like social media integration, mobile donations, and virtual events to expand their reach and impact, while sophisticated data analytics track donor behavior and campaign effectiveness, optimizing future efforts.

In order to thrive in today's market, businesses simply have to find a way to deliver working software solutions, as quickly and as reliably as possible. Traditional development methodologies often lead to long development cycles, increased costs, and delayed time to market, which can be hugely detrimental. This emphasis on technology isn't going away any time soon. A recent Gartner report found that 61% of businesses plan to increase their investment in technology in 2024.

Unfortunately though, delivering the kind of reliable, high-quality software that can help an organization to thrive—particularly consistently, or at pace—is a really difficult job. Most organizations will have to change the way they deliver software if they wish to achieve this.

Continuous integration (CI) and continuous deployment (CD) emerged in the early 2000s as part of the Agile movement. Today, they are standard practice for high-performing development teams worldwide. Companies like Amazon, Google, Netflix, Tesla, and PayPal all practice

CI/CD in various forms. These practices enable these companies to maintain a competitive edge by delivering new features, improvements, and innovations to their customers rapidly and reliably.

Continuous Integration

CI describes the art of continuously merging your code in small increments and running it through your CI pipeline each time, so as to make sure that every developer's changes will continue to work when it's all brought together and deployed to the end user. It involves each developer continuously merging their commits into the main branch where a suite of tests and checks run automatically on their code, assuring that everything in that main branch still meets the required standard for production. This process ensures that every developer's changes work together harmoniously.

This process of integrating code changes frequently, multiple times a day, helps teams identify and address any integration issues nice and early, leading to much more stable codebases and a much faster feedback loop for developers working on the codebase. This feedback loop is crucial as it enables developers to quickly learn about the impact their changes will have on the overall system, allowing them to make necessary adjustments before those changes cause even bigger issues downstream and ultimately leading to a more stable codebase. When developers can find integration issues early and frequently, they can also fix them early and frequently!

In practical terms, CI involves using tools like Jenkins, Travis CI, or GitHub Actions to automate the process of integrating changes. These tools build and test each change automatically, ensure that the new code does not introduce bugs or break existing functionality, and run any other checks that are needed to ensure the branch is ready for end users. This automation significantly reduces the risk of human error, which is a common cause of integration problems in more traditional, manual processes.

A well-implemented CI process will include various types of testing to ensure quality. Unit tests, which test individual components of the software, are run to ensure that each part of the codebase works as expected. Integration tests verify that different components of the system work together seamlessly. And end-to-end tests simulate real user scenarios to ensure that the application functions correctly from the end user's perspective.

By integrating changes frequently, developers are also more likely to discuss and resolve issues together, leading to a more collaborative culture that should help foster an environment that allows for high-performing development teams to flourish. This collaborative environment helps foster innovation and continuous improvement as team members learn from each other.

Continuous Deployment

CD describes the process of deploying your code or code artifacts into your test environments and through to your production (as well as your non-production, test environments) after your CI checks pass. This production deployment can happen automatically, without any manual intervention at all, meaning that after you merge, your code will immediately be on the path to production to start serving users. This swift transition from code commit to deployment ensures that the latest changes are available to users as quickly as possible. You'll need a robust pipeline and automated checks to confirm your software is in a releasable state, but you can reduce the opportunity for human error in the release process, minimize risk, and ultimately speed up your entire software delivery processes.

These automated deployment processes enable development teams to focus on coding and improving the application rather than getting bogged down in the minutiae of deployment tasks. CD aims to streamline the whole process between commit and deployment, reduce time to market, encourage smaller batch releases, and increase the efficiency of development teams, all by automating as much as possible.

As with CI, the faster feedback loops you can achieve from CD, as changes are quickly pushed to production and served to real users, also allow for more rapid iteration of your software and processes. This rapid feedback is critical because it enables teams to detect and address real, live issues as quickly in the software development lifecycle as possible, ensuring higher-quality and more reliable software.

Continuous Delivery

We also use the acronym CD to describe a similar but slightly different process in continuous delivery. This is similar to continuous deployment in that every change you integrate into the main branch is then built as a production-ready application. The major difference with continuous delivery is that the application isn't then required to be actually deployed to real users automatically. The decision on whether or not to deploy this change to production is ultimately manual and is left up to a decision by a human on the team.

Continuous delivery—rather than continuous deployment—can be useful for applications that can't be deployed often or for which deploying often might actually be quite inconvenient. This might be the case, for example, for applications designed for commercial consumption by other businesses, where you don't want to support multiple versions of an application simultaneously. Similarly, continuous delivery might be more practical for embedded driver software, software running on mainframe systems, or mobile apps. In these scenarios, managing multiple versions might add significant load to the development team's workload, or perhaps deploying frequently might even disrupt or annoy your end users. If you can deploy your change immediately, I'd urge you to do so. But for those use cases where it really isn't feasible, you can still get huge benefits from continuous delivery.

Continuous delivery ensures that your software is always in a deployable state. This means that while the deployment might not be automated, the application has still been tested and verified as if it were going to be deployed and ultimately is ready to be deployed at any time. This approach provides extra flexibility and control over the deployment process compared with continuous deployment, allowing teams to choose the optimal time for release based on business needs, user readiness, and other considerations, but this ability to defer the deployment decision must not detract from the discipline and rigor of ensuring that every build is of production quality. Continuous delivery should simply add a layer of strategic deployment planning, not allow you to in any way compromise the quality of the code that ends up in your main branch.

Embracing CD methodologies, whether continuous deployment or continuous delivery, positions organizations to respond in a more agile way to market changes, user feedback, and technological advancements. The iterative nature of these processes fosters an environment of continuous improvement, where teams can rapidly release new features, fix bugs, and optimize their performance. The reduced time to market for new features not only enhances user satisfaction but also provides a competitive edge in fast-paced industries where staying ahead of the curve is absolutely crucial.

For some organizations though, this shift to continuous deployment or continuous delivery represents a significant cultural and operational change. It requires robust automated testing frameworks, thorough monitoring, and a culture of accountability among development teams. Teams must be prepared to own their code through its lifecycle, from commit to deployment and beyond, including post-deployment monitoring and quick rollback procedures if issues arise.

Continuous deployment and continuous delivery are both powerful methodologies that transform the way software is developed, tested, and released. Whether deploying automatically or manually, the benefits of these practices are clear; they drive better outcomes for both development teams and end users.

Why Do We Do CI/CD?

So why is any of this worth doing at all anyway, I hear you ask. Is this all just some concept that techie folk have made up to entertain themselves? The answer is, of course, no. CI/CD are concepts we follow for the benefit of our end users and to aid in the success of the organization we work for.

Imagine a world with long-lived feature branches, slow testing and slow release cycles, a change review board, manual regression testing, a sign-off process before production releases, and manual deployments. I'm sure many of you reading have enough experience in the industry such that you might not even have to use your imagination for this scenario! This team may believe themselves to be driven by quality and the art of being super-super-careful. Perhaps they feel that they would be much more prone to disastrous bugs were they to cut any of their heavy quality assurance processes. Perhaps they feel, because every time they deploy to production they have major problems, that deploying to production more often would lead to even greater problems. This logic sort of does make intuitive sense to them, and so maybe it strengthens them in their current ways of working even further, and these heavy processes around the path to production become even more complex and cumbersome.

In the above scenario, the team may be tempted to put five, six, maybe seven tickets through this complicated and slow release process all together as one. And, in all fairness, this does feel like an efficient way to deal with a massively slow release process, rather than going through that process separately seven distinct times. But that creates more problems— there are now seven different pieces of work where we might find bugs or missed requirements. And what happens if and when we do find these problems? Who is responsible for fixing them? What if these problems have come about because of the way the different changes in two different tickets have come together, rather than being the fault of one change?

This release process has probably become so complicated by this point that the team needs some kind of release manager or perhaps just a poor developer or QA acting as a sort of unofficial release manager. Perhaps this release manager is responsible for merging and batching all of these tickets together. Perhaps they're also responsible for triaging any problems with releases and then trying to find the best, least busy developer, with the most context possible, to look into it. But then what? Does the whole release now wait while this developer takes the time away from their day job to look into this new bug? Do we try to revert some of the broken code out of this release candidate and leave the rest of the tickets to go through to production? Does this mean the testing cycle for this release starts from the beginning?

CI/CD makes the above situation significantly simpler and more straightforward. Releases should absolutely not be—and with a good CI/CD approach are not—a big deal in any way. When a developer makes a code change, they get that change reviewed as immediately as possible by another developer and then merge their code to go immediately straight through to production. They are then responsible for monitoring their change in production, including adding any observability, logging, or extra metrics their change might need, and they are then responsible for keeping an eye out for any problems caused by the code they've merged and deployed. They're also responsible for reverting or fixing their change if there are problems.

In this new CI/CD world, you can release to production after every single change. If a change does cause issues, a developer will already have all the context they need fresh in their mind. And actually, only one change is happening at a time, so it is much less likely anything will go wrong with each release! Every release to production is smaller and therefore safer. It allows you to keep your work in progress (WIP) low—improving focus and productivity and improving your team's cycle time.

The transformation brought about by CI/CD practices cannot be overstated. By eliminating the lengthy and cumbersome processes associated with traditional software development cycles, teams can shift their focus to innovation and improvement. Continuous integration and continuous deployment ensure that code is always in a deployable state and that every change, no matter how minor, is automatically tested and verified. This results in higher-quality software and issues that are identified and resolved as early as possible in the development process.

Moreover, the immediate feedback loop provided by CI/CD means that developers can learn and adapt quickly. When a change is merged, it is instantly tested and, if it passes, it is deployed to production. If their change fails, the developer receives immediate feedback and can address the issue right away. This rapid iteration cycle leads to a more agile development process, where changes can be made and tested in real time.

For businesses, the benefits of adopting CI/CD are significant. Faster release cycles mean that new features and updates reach customers more quickly. This ability to respond rapidly to user feedback ensures that the software evolves in line with customer needs and market demands, driving organizational success. High-performing teams who follow the principles of CI/CD are statistically more likely to achieve success for their organization.

CI/CD also inherently reduces risk. By automating the testing and deployment processes, the chance of human error is minimized. Automated and consistent checks and balances ensure that only changes that meet predefined quality standards are deployed to production.

In the context of team dynamics, CI/CD fosters a culture of collaboration and accountability. Developers take ownership of their code through to production and take on the responsibility for its successful deployment to the end user. No more is this the job of a sad and stressed release manager with no context of the change. This accountability drives higher standards of quality and encourages continuous improvement. Teams work together more effectively, as the barriers between development, testing, and operations are broken down, leading to a more cohesive and efficient workflow.

So the adoption of CI/CD is not just a technical enhancement but a fundamental shift in the way software is developed and delivered. It streamlines processes, improves software quality, accelerates time to market, and enhances customer satisfaction. By embracing CI/CD, organizations can stay ahead of the competition, responding rapidly to changing market conditions and continuously delivering quality software.

Ultimately, the reason we are building software and writing code in the first place is to deliver value to our users, whoever our users may be. The shorter release cycles allowed by CI and CD ensure that new features and updates can be delivered to users much, much quicker and also allow for fast responses to user feedback and needs. Instead of waiting for the next release cycle, in which a change might be blocked by a complicated testing cycle on a completely different part of the application written by a completely different developer, you can now deploy a feature which delivers customer value the same day you finish development on it.

The Science Behind CI/CD

"Is this safe?" is the question most business people—and even a few technology professionals—ask when you talk to them about CI/CD, particularly CD. The answer, of course, is yes. Not only is it totally safe, but it will also provide significant benefits to your business.

It may feel counterintuitive to some that removing manual tests and checks from a process can make it safer and more efficient. And CI/CD does indeed require a high degree of trust in your CI pipeline and automated test suite, but there is a great deal of evidence that suggests a move toward repeatable, consistent, automated build and deploy pipelines can be of great benefit to any organization.

As technologists, we can perhaps more easily see the virtues of CI/CD, but it may seem counterintuitive to our colleagues in other parts of the business that moving faster and releasing more often is actually safer and more reliable. This can be a particularly challenging sell if you're part of a team that has struggled with big deployments in the past. I have certainly joined teams myself that have been investing massive amounts of time, effort, and planning into huge releases, putting them through heavy manual testing cycles that last many weeks. And then, even after all that effort, their big release might (and probably will) throw up showstopping bugs in production, requiring days of firefighting and potentially costing their company money.

How do you sell the idea to such a team that it would be much safer for them to release 20 times a day? They'll probably look at you as if you're mad. You might even start to doubt yourself! Maybe after watching a few of their large unsuccessful deployments you'll start to believe that, for this specific use case and this level of complexity, CI/CD simply won't work. Their service is too big, or it's too complicated, or it isn't modern enough, perhaps. Maybe there is too much regulation or bureaucracy because this team works in financial services or the government. The good news is that CI/CD can be applied and have great benefit, not just across industries but also for pretty much any type of software.

One of the most compelling aspects of CI/CD is its ability to reduce the risk of deployment failures, like the failures the team in the above example are running into. By deploying smaller, incremental changes more frequently, teams can catch and fix issues early. This approach contrasts sharply with the traditional model of infrequent, large releases, where issues are harder to pinpoint and resolve and where there are much more of them.

For instance, imagine a team that deploys once every few months. The amount of code changes, new features, and bug fixes bundled into that release is substantial, any part of that code could have issues, and it's very difficult to isolate the cause of any problems that arise. In contrast, a team deploying multiple times a day deals with smaller, more manageable sets of changes. If an issue occurs, it's easier to identify the recent change that caused it, making debugging faster and more efficient and rollbacks much more straightforward.

The automation inherent in CI/CD processes also minimizes human error. Automated tests and checks ensure that each code change meets quality standards before it is merged and deployed. This automation not only increases efficiency but also provides a consistent and reliable way to verify the integrity of your software.

Addressing the skepticism of teams accustomed to traditional deployment methods involves demonstrating all of these practical benefits and leveraging the wealth of research available. One effective strategy I've found is to start small, perhaps with a pilot project, to showcase how CI/CD can improve reliability and speed without compromising safety.

For example, in highly regulated industries such as financial services or the government, it might seem daunting to adopt CI/CD due to strict compliance requirements. However, with the right approach, CI/CD can help automate and enhance your existing compliance process by ensuring that every change is tracked, tested, and documented automatically. By incorporating compliance checks into the CI/CD pipeline, teams can ensure that regulatory requirements are met consistently and efficiently without risk of human error.

Implementing CI/CD does also require a shift in mindset. Teams need to embrace automation and continuous improvement, focusing on building a robust CI/CD pipeline that can handle the demands of these frequent deployments. They might be more willing to come along on that ride if they can see and buy into the success of your "pilot."

CI/CD shouldn't just be a one-time implementation but an ongoing journey for the team. Teams should continuously evaluate and refine their processes, leveraging feedback from each deployment to identify areas for improvement. The whole team needs to be bought in for this to work.

The transition to CI/CD may require a cultural shift and a commitment to continuous learning, but the rewards are definitely well worth the effort. By embracing automation, continuous improvement, and a robust CI/CD pipeline, teams can achieve more reliable software, faster deployments, and, ultimately, better business outcomes. While it may seem counterintuitive, the evidence from research and practical experience supports the benefits of adopting CI/CD practices.

Indeed, there is even peer-reviewed research (such as research carried out by the DevOps Research and Assessment (DORA) research program) telling us that CI/CD leads not only to more reliable software with fewer bugs but to a higher chance of organizational success.

DevOps Research and Assessment (DORA)

DORA (DevOps Research and Assessment) is a research program founded by Dr. Nicole Forsgren, Jez Humble, and Gene Kim and acquired by Google in 2018. The primary goal of DORA is to apply rigorous academic, peer-reviewed research to the field of software delivery performance, providing data-driven insights into the most effective ways to deliver software. Since its inception, DORA has been at the forefront of researching and understanding the intricacies of software development and deployment and has transformed the way organizations understand, measure, and improve their software delivery processes.

The DORA research and reports are rooted in empirical data, which means they are based on observations and experiences rather than purely theoretical constructs. This empirical approach provides a solid foundation for the insights and recommendations offered by DORA, making them highly reliable and applicable in real-world scenarios. Their research does a fantastic job at bridging the gap between academic research and practical application in the software industry.

One of the outcomes of DORA's research are the famous DORA metrics. These are a set of key performance indicators, based on DORA research, that can be used to measure the effectiveness and efficiency of a team's software delivery processes. These metrics focus on four primary areas: deployment frequency, lead time for changes, mean time to recovery (MTTR), and change failure rate. Deployment frequency measures how often new code is deployed to production, reflecting the agility of the development process. Lead time for changes indicates the time taken from code commit to deployment, showcasing the speed of delivery. Mean time to recovery tracks the time required to restore service after an incident, highlighting the resilience and reliability of a team and their platform. Change failure rate assesses the percentage of deployments that cause failures in production, highlighting the quality and stability of a team's releases. All together, these metrics can help provide a comprehensive view of a team's performance.

One of DORA's other most significant contributions to the field are its annual State of DevOps reports. These reports, first published in 2014, have become a brilliant resource for software development teams worldwide, and I strongly suggest you give them a read. The reports are based on extensive surveys and data collection efforts, involving thousands of respondents from diverse industries across the world. This comprehensive dataset allows DORA to identify trends, challenges, and best practices in software delivery with a high degree of confidence. The State of DevOps reports provide a wealth of information on various aspects of software delivery, including technical practices, team dynamics, and organizational culture. One of the key findings from these reports, of course, is the critical role of CI/CD in achieving high performance in software delivery.

The 2023 State of DevOps report describes continuous delivery (CD) as "a substantial mediator of many technical capabilities," meaning that other technical capabilities correlated with high-performing organizations seem to be beneficial mainly because they make CD possible. For instance, practices such as automated testing, infrastructure as code (IaC), and trunk-based development all contribute to the ability to deliver software continuously. High-performing teams who follow these practices are able to integrate and deploy their code multiple times a day, significantly reducing the time it takes to get new features and fixes to users.

There is also plenty of robust empirical evidence supporting the benefits of continuous delivery in these reports over the years. In their book *Accelerate*, the founders of DORA delve deeper into some of the detailed statistics from their research. They highlight findings in their research that continuous delivery not only enhances performance but also leads to higher-quality software. One of the critical findings, for example, is that continuous delivery "predicts lower levels of unplanned work and rework in a statistically significant way" (*Accelerate*, p. 47), highlighting the efficiency gains a team gets from adopting CD. These high-performing teams, as identified by DORA, have 11% more of their time to spend on new work, rather than bug fixes, emergency deployments, patches, etc. Essentially, teams practicing continuous delivery spend more time on new development rather than firefighting issues. This shift allows for a more innovative and forward-thinking approach, where teams can focus on delivering improvements rather than being bogged down by maintenance tasks and fixing incidents.

The 2017 DORA report further underscores the benefits of continuous delivery by revealing that high-performing teams deploy 46 times more frequently than their low-performing counterparts. This increased deployment frequency is not just about pushing code to production more often; it reflects a fundamental shift in how these teams operate. Frequent deployments mean that changes are smaller and more manageable, reducing the risk of large, disruptive changes. This, in turn, leads to statistically fewer failures—high-performing teams experience five times fewer failures when they do make changes. Additionally, if failures do occur, these teams recover 96 times faster than low-performing teams. This rapid recovery is crucial in maintaining user trust and minimizing downtime, which can have significant financial implications. And it all comes about by taking a better approach to deploying and rolling back code and making a change in the way development teams approach production issues.

Beyond the technical and quality improvements, DORA's findings also indicate that organizations classified as high or elite performers in software delivery are up to twice as likely to achieve their organizational goals. These goals include profitability, customer satisfaction, and market share, highlighting the broader business benefits of adopting CI/CD practices.

This finding highlights that effective software delivery is absolutely not just a technical concern but actually also a strategic business advantage for the organization as a whole. Organizations that implement continuous delivery practices are better positioned to respond faster to market changes and customer feedback. They deploy new features more quickly, allowing them to adapt to user needs and stay ahead of competitors. And they have the ability to deploy frequently and recover quickly from failures. All of this means that these organizations have the time and space to experiment more freely and drive innovations and big technological improvements. So these aren't just stats for tech nerds. Teams who perform well by these measures don't just perform better technically; their wider organizations are also statistically more likely to achieve success.

The empirical data gathered and analyzed by DORA should offer a roadmap for organizations looking to transform their software delivery practices and achieve higher performance levels and can be used to show that following CI/CD practices aren't just something to be done for technical reasons, but actually should be done because it will allow your organization to be more likely to make more money.

Of course, it isn't just DORA shouting about the huge benefits of CD. The 2023 LeadDev report also reinforces the importance of CI/CD, identifying it as one of the essential tools that enable development teams to excel. The report notes that 57% of engineering managers surveyed cited CI/CD as one of the tools that allows development teams to do their best work. This is a significant endorsement, as it reflects the practical benefits observed by those directly managing and working within these teams. Sixty-five percent of respondents also cited DORA metrics as a tool they'd found useful for measuring team performance. These metrics can provide a clear and objective way to assess how well teams are performing, allowing for continuous improvement driven from real data.

Key Takeaways

- **Importance of Software in Business:** Software is critical across various industries, from retail to oil, music, and charity, enabling organizations to operate efficiently and stay competitive.

- **Continuous Integration (CI):** CI is the practice of merging code changes frequently into a shared repository, ensuring that all developers' contributions work harmoniously. Automated testing and checks are crucial components, enabling early identification and resolution of integration issues, leading to a more stable codebase and faster feedback loops.

- **Continuous Deployment (CD):** CD is the act of automatically deploying code to production once it passes CI checks. This process minimizes human error, speeds up the software delivery process, and allows for rapid iterations based on real-time user feedback. CD might also stand for continuous delivery, where deployment is manual but the main branch is always in a production-ready state.

- **Cultural Shift:** Adopting CI/CD requires a significant cultural shift, fostering a collaborative environment where developers take full ownership of their code from development through production. It emphasizes automation, reducing manual interventions and improving overall efficiency and quality.

- **Benefits of CI/CD:** The adoption of CI/CD practices leads to faster release cycles, higher software quality, and a competitive edge in the market. It reduces risks associated with large, infrequent releases by promoting smaller, incremental changes.

- **DORA Metrics:** Deployment frequency, lead time for changes, mean time to recovery, and change failure rate are key indicators of CI/CD success. High-performing teams, as identified by DORA research, are more likely to achieve better business outcomes.

- **Empirical Evidence:** Research strongly supports the adoption of CI/CD for its significant benefits, including improved reliability, efficiency, and its impact on organizational success.

In the next chapter we will discuss the fundamental building blocks of CI/CD, covering the basic foundations of these practices.

CHAPTER 2

The Fundamentals of CI/CD

Unfortunately, transitioning to CI/CD is not as straightforward as merely creating a brand-new build and deploy pipeline and then going ahead and deploying any software you have straight to production. There are a number of foundational elements you might want to consider carefully before just jumping straight into things headfirst. It's important to note that while CI/CD will definitely allow you to move more quickly and streamline your development process, you must first ensure you put the right foundations in place to allow you to do this all safely and in a way that allows your transition to this new way of working to be smooth and effective!

By carefully considering and implementing these foundational elements though, you can ensure a smooth journey to CI/CD, and the benefits of faster delivery cycles, improved quality, and greater agility are well worth the effort of laying these solid foundations. In the following sections, we will delve deeper into some of these elements, providing best practices and practical advice to help you successfully implement CI/CD in your organization.

© Tommy Clark 2025
T. Clark, *CI/CD Unleashed*, Apress Pocket Guides,
https://doi.org/10.1007/979-8-8688-1209-5_2

Testing

Testing is one, if not the most, absolutely foundational tenet of both continuous integration and continuous delivery. If you cannot trust that your automated test suite is acting as a reliable indicator of the health and quality of your application, it is very hard to see if your efforts to integrate have been successful in an automated, consistent, and efficient way. This can be a particularly difficult pill to swallow when tackling legacy codebases, as it is so much more difficult to write tests as an afterthought, compared with applications where testing has been baked into the development process from the start. Either way, greenfield or legacy, your automated test suite is king!

You can gain a lot of advantages in terms of ways of working if you can ensure that every change made to the codebase is validated against a comprehensive suite of tests that verify the functionality, performance, and security of your application and can give you a reliable indicator on whether your application has passed your quality threshold for moving into production.

This consistent, efficient, repeatable, and reliable validation process can be absolutely essential for maintaining the integrity of your software, especially as the codebase grows and evolves over time. Without automated tests, developers and QA engineers would have to manually check each change, which is both time-consuming and prone to human error. A fast and consistent way to verify that your software works as intended can be absolutely indispensable on the journey to delivering continuous integration and continuous delivery.

In the context of legacy codebases though, the challenge of implementing automated tests can be really great. Legacy systems often have complex interdependencies, lack proper documentation, and may not have been designed with testability in mind. Writing tests for such systems requires a thorough understanding of the existing code, identifying critical functionalities, and developing tests that cover these areas without disrupting the current operations. This process can be painstaking, but it is crucial for ensuring that the legacy system can be safely integrated into a CI/CD pipeline. The effort invested in creating an automated test suite for a legacy codebase pays off by significantly reducing the risk of introducing bugs during integration, deployment, and future refactors. I've found it helpful on projects like this to start off with high-level end-to-end tests, which test the core functionality of the application in a way that gives you and your QA team a fair amount of confidence. If this application is currently being deployed regularly, it's important to analyze the quality checks that currently block this application's journey to production and audit exactly how much of this could be automated away.

For greenfield projects, integrating automated testing from the start is much simpler and much more effective. By adopting practices like test-driven development (TDD), teams can ensure that tests are written before the actual code is written at all, making the code itself inherently more testable and reliable. TDD encourages writing small, incremental tests that validate specific functionalities, leading to a really robust test suite that grows alongside the codebase. This approach not only ensures high test coverage but also promotes good design practices, as the code is constantly being written to meet the requirements of your automated tests.

The importance of a reliable automated test suite cannot be overstated. It serves as the first line of defense against bugs and regressions, catching issues early in the development cycle before they escalate into bigger problems. Developers should be running these tests against their code locally every single time they make a change, allowing them to receive feedback almost instantly and enabling them to identify and fix issues promptly. This rapid feedback loop is essential for maintaining the momentum of continuous integration and continuous delivery and allows teams to release new features and updates more frequently and confidently.

Developers working on a platform with a strong test suite are also able to confidently work on new and different parts of the codebase and have the confidence that their changes will be validated against a strong set of tests. This consistency helps prevent integration conflicts and ensures that the code remains in a good and stable state, even as multiple developers contribute to the project simultaneously.

Ultimately, the goal of automated testing in CI/CD is to create that reliable, repeatable, and efficient process for validating software changes. It provides the confidence needed to integrate and deploy code frequently and therefore reduces time to market and improves the overall quality of your application. Whether working with legacy systems or new projects, investing in a robust automated test suite is absolutely key to continuous integration and continuous delivery.

Test-Driven Development

So how do you bake testing into your development process? Test-driven development is a term coined by Kent Beck and described in his 2002 book—*Test Driven Development: By Example*. Since then, it has become an integral way in which high-performing software development teams operate and write code.

TDD is an approach in which your unit tests are continuously written before your actual application code. The process follows a simple, repetitive cycle: red/green/refactor. Firstly, write a small test outlining the next bit of functionality you want to add to your codebase and then run it, watching your test go red. Then, write the minimum amount of functional code possible in order to make the test pass (i.e., go green). Finally, refactor both your new and old code to make it readable and well structured. You then start the process again for your next piece of functionality and again for your next piece of functionality. Et voila! You are now performing test-driven development! This red/green/refactor TDD cycle was designed to enable developers to write clean units of code that they are absolutely confident will and do work.

This process leads to very good test coverage of the functionality of your code, giving any developers working on code related to this functionality in the future confidence that they won't break anything or cause unintended side effects with their own change.

But TDD doesn't just lead to good-quality test coverage. TDD was designed to lead to code that is clearer, simpler, and bug-free, thus improving the overall quality of the software. Test-driven development encourages you to design and write your code in single, testable units, leading to more easily readable and better-quality codebases. It also means that after you've written a unit of code, you have tests describing the precise expected outputs of that code given a particular input. This not only makes future refactoring easy, but it also allows your unit tests to act as living, breathing pieces of documentation outlining the current functionality of the code they sit alongside.

Developers naturally produce more modular and decoupled code following this process, which is crucial for maintaining and scaling the application over time. When components are well-defined and self-contained, it becomes much easier to make changes, add new features, or troubleshoot issues without any inadvertent effects.

TDD also helps foster a culture of accountability and thoroughness among developers. Since tests are written first, developers must clearly understand the requirements and expected behavior of their code before implementation and discuss these requirements in more detail if they find that they do not. This forward-thinking approach reduces the likelihood of misunderstandings, missed requirements, or overlooked edge cases, leading to more robust and reliable software.

The iterative nature of TDD—red/green/refactor—also means that refactoring is a built-in part of the cycle, so code is being continuously improved and optimized. This practice helps keep the code readable and maintainable.

TDD can also help enhance team collaboration, knowledge sharing, and onboarding, due to the tests serving as a form of living documentation that are always inherently correct and up-to-date. When new team members join or when developers need to work on different parts of the codebase, these tests provide valuable insights into how the system is supposed to function in that area. This shared understanding helps team members onboard and get up to scratch quickly and effectively.

All of this enables continuous integration for teams. With TDD, developers can frequently refactor and change the code confidently, knowing that any introduced defects will be quickly caught by the unit tests in their continuous integration pipeline. CI/CD ultimately requires software changes to seem utterly non-scary to developers! And good-quality test coverage gives developers the freedom to improve and modify code without fear. This all leads to a final product that is robust, reliable, quick to iterate on, and, ultimately, more likely to meet the user's needs.

The confidence that TDD provides extends to the deployment phase too. Knowing that your code is well-tested means you can deploy changes more frequently and with greater assurance that they won't disrupt the system. This confidence is the absolute cornerstone of continuous delivery and deployment practices, where the goal is to get new features and fixes to users as quickly and safely as possible.

Testing generally, and specifically test-driven development, is not just a technical practice but a cultural shift toward quality and reliability. It transforms how teams think about and write code, leading to better products and more efficient development processes.

The Testing Pyramid

Even if you have followed TDD and you have a strong suite of unit tests covering 100% of your code, how are you to know for sure that your application is working as expected? Different units of code might integrate with each other in an unexpected way or call each other in a different way from the way your unit tests work. The test data in your unit test might not be realistic or reflective of the variety of data your application experiences in production. Your frontend code might be well unit tested, but look strange in a particular browser or be affected in production by a specific external dependency. Frankly speaking, relying on *just* unit tests simply isn't going to cut it.

So what else do we need to do to have a reliable and useful indicator that our application is in a working state?

In 2009, Mike Cohn described the testing pyramid in his book *Succeeding with Agile*. He proposed that unit tests are indeed the foundation of a solid automation test strategy and at the base of what he calls the test automation pyramid. Unit tests are low cost, specific to the unit of a code a developer might be working on, and quick to run, and so we can have as many of them as we need. Developers may well be writing units of code and running the unit tests alongside that code 50–100 times a day. And as unit tests are the base of the pyramid, this means we want as much coverage as we can get from our unit tests. But they aren't the only tool in your arsenal when automating your test coverage.

At the very top of the pyramid are user interface (UI) tests. UI tests are inherently slower and more brittle than a unit test. They rely on clicking around a UI in a browser and so take time to run and are at the mercy of all sorts of factors that might cause even the best and most valid test of the most perfectly working application to fail. They're also more expensive and time-consuming to create in a way that is reliable and valuable in the long run. You can write UI tests using capture and replay tools, and they're much cheaper to create, but they are generally less reliable. That isn't to say UI tests are useless—far from it—but they shouldn't be testing every branch of logic in your codebase. UI tests should be light-touch and testing just the key journeys, hence sitting at the top of the pyramid.

If the top of the pyramid is just light-touch testing of the key journeys exactly as your user would see them and the bottom of the pyramid is testing specific, small, standalone units of code, how do we test the different complex branches of logic across the application? This is where the middle of the pyramid comes in.

The middle of the pyramid is occupied by service or integration tests. These tests are critical in verifying the seamless interaction between different parts of your application. They can assess the communication between databases, servers, and APIs, ensuring they all work together as harmoniously as they were intended to. Unlike unit tests, which examine small individual components in isolation, integration tests are less granular. They do not focus on single components but rather on how these component parts of the software all work together. The advantage they have over end-to-end UI tests is that they're going to be much faster and more reliable, and so you can have a lot more of them in your test suite without causing issues with reliability or speed.

To give you an idea by way of example, the top of your pyramid is a UI test in Playwright testing login to your website with a working username and password, the middle might be a Karate test to test what happens if you log into the website with an incorrect username or password or maybe testing for SQL injection, for example, while the very bottom of the pyramid would be many small, quick unit tests covering every piece of functionality to do with login, testing every different potential input to each field (spaces, unusual characters, too many or few characters, etc.).

Figure 2-1 illustrates how the testing pyramid is laid out.

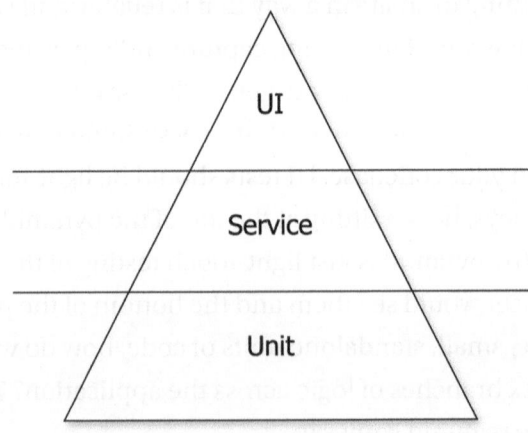

Figure 2-1. *The testing pyramid*

Following the testing pyramid is more likely to give you reliable indicators of the quality of your application and allow the whole suite of tests to run at speed, which will allow you to run them in your deployment pipeline. Blocking the path to production with flaky, slow tests is not a helpful practice. CD is about speeding a team up, not slowing them down, and teams will start to ignore intermittent failures if they happen too often.

Any test failures in your main branch should be priority number one for the development team! The team should instantly swarm on any test failures happening in the main branch of your codebase. What is perhaps less obvious though is that slow and flaky tests need to be picked up as priority too. If a test is flaky and fails regularly and can't be fixed, how useful is it? It may even be better to delete it entirely. If a slow test can't be made faster, perhaps that test has been written on the wrong level of the testing pyramid. The path to production must be as fast and reliable as possible.

Testing More Than Just Code

Testing your software isn't just about testing the application code you've written though! Continuous deployment requires confidence in any change to your codebase that is going to be deployed through to production.

In addition to your functional tests, automated testing should also encompass, for example, performance and/or security QA checks. Performance tests can help ensure that the application can handle your expected load profiles and perform efficiently under various conditions. Security tests can identify vulnerabilities and ensure that your application is resilient against potential threats. By integrating these tests into the CI/CD pipeline, teams can ensure that the software meets all quality and security standards before being deployed to production.

Luckily, if you're using CD, then running your pipeline is the only way to get your change live, so you know exactly where to check for any blockers for releasing any part of your codebase.

Perhaps you work in an industry where performance under heavy traffic is incredibly important, and so you need to load test your code before release to make sure any changes haven't damaged user flows in any way or broken any service-level objectives (SLOs) or service-level agreements (SLAs) other application teams may have on your services.

Perhaps you also want dependency auditing, to make sure that every change has the latest stable versions of every dependency you pull in. Your pipeline is the one and only route to production, so again it is the perfect place to do it!

You may also want to add steps into your pipeline to make sure that, as a team, you're not compromising on quality. Static analysis tools, like SonarQube, can automatically scan your code for any "smells," code styling issues, or potential security problems and calculate the complexity of your code and give you tips as to whether certain classes or functions should be broken down. You should also consider scanning for vulnerabilities and security issues before releasing any new code, using Orca, Dependabot, snyk, npm audit, or any one of the many off-the-shelf tools available.

What If We Don't Have Automated Tests?

A lot of the time, teams are nervous about continuously deploying to production. Their fear is that, without lots and lots of extra automated testing, they will have no idea whether their code is actually safe for production or not. The problem with that way of thinking is that it's very difficult to "catch up" and cover every single test case in a complex, living system, which in turn means you may never get to the point where you can start to reap any of the benefits of CD. Catching up on covering all of your functionality, while new functionality is still being built in the background, can feel like changing the tires on a moving car.

In my experience however, there are some compromises that can be made with regard to manual testing and parts of the code that don't yet have automated tests in place. For example, you might consider whether you can still theoretically keep all of the same QA and testing that you're doing currently, but carry this same process out before you merge into your main branch rather than after. A number of development teams I've worked with in the past that are moving toward CI/CD processes have found great value in creating prod-like integrated environments that they can deploy a branch or multiple branches to in order to test tickets manually before deploying them. This manual testing should still be as light-touch as possible, and we should always look for ways to automate these tests eventually, but this process can allow you to start to feel some of the benefits of CI/CD quicker. You are then free to iterate on this process while at least receiving some of the benefits of CI/CD.

Picture a development team that relies wholly on manual testing (perhaps they have some unit tests or automated test suites maintained by a central QA team, but they don't use these tests as a reliable indicator as to the quality of the code). This team might have three or four branches for three or four tickets, all being worked on by different developers. When these developers are done with their features, they might let a QA team know they're finished. The QA team might collect together all three or four tickets and merge them into the main branch. At this point, the main branch is full of untested code that is not ready for production. They might then put this code through a one- to two-week manual testing cycle, testing all of the known functionality of the application. If they have bugs, they might triage these bugs and find the most suitable developer to work on it. That developer might take a couple of days to fix the bug, at which point the QA team might merge this bug in and put the application through another one- to two-week manual testing cycle. In the meantime, perhaps four, five, or six other pull requests (PRs) for long-lived branches have been opened, all sitting around becoming stale, waiting for the QA team to action them. The workflow of this application has become a confusing and convoluted mess.

Even in the situation above, you can massively simplify things and move toward the principles of CI by making sure you avoid the pitfalls of having your main branch become a place where you integrate a bunch of untested code. You can do this by simply doing all of your manual testing in your branch, before you merge. Even if a team does then still rely on some manual testing in certain cases, CI allows branches that do have automated test coverage to be merged straight away (or at least much quicker) avoiding long-lived stale feature branches as much as possible and also allows the main branch to be the source of truth and a place for tested, production-ready code, simplifying the workflow hugely and hopefully speeding the entire team up.

Your QA team should be kept in the loop the entire time. They should be consulting on the best way to test the functionality of each ticket. And while also helping out with the direction of your automated test suite, they should be able to advise exactly what needs to be done to test a ticket pre-merge to allow it to go into the main branch and straight through to production. If there is reluctance, simply ask what testing would need to be carried out in the current workflow and figure out how to either automate this away or cover it with manual testing in the branch in the short term.

While continuous deployment without extensive automated testing is far from ideal and the fear of doing so is not entirely misplaced, I do think it is important to recognize that catching up on tests for a complex system can be impractical. Instead, you may want to consider integrating manual testing earlier in the process, using prod-like environments, and progressively building a comprehensive automated test suite can help your team transition to CI/CD slowly. By maintaining a stable main branch with tested, production-ready code and leveraging tools and practices that facilitate continuous integration, teams can achieve faster, safer, and more efficient deployments. A move toward CI/CD should always be measured and iterative, just like software development.

Manual Testing

Automated testing doesn't mean that manual testing is completely pointless—far from it! This type of testing might help find issues with usability of your application, might help find missing test cases (which can then be automated at the correct level of the testing pyramid), and can help find missing or misunderstood requirements during development.

What automation does mean is that you can focus your manual testing efforts in places where it is a more useful tool. Manual testing is an expensive, slow, and extremely unreliable way to regression test an application after every feature or change, and these sorts of regression tests should absolutely be automated as a priority. But manual testing can still be of use to a team as a tool for exploratory testing.

Your QA will have a really thorough understanding of the wider requirements of your application and the behavior of your users, and so ultimately they're best placed to spot where a developer has overlooked a requirement or misinterpreted a ticket. The human element of manual testing also allows a tester to approach the application with fresh eyes, uncovering usability issues not easily covered by automated scripts.

Don't discount manual testing as one of the tools in your toolbox—just don't have it be a blocker for the path to production.

Small Frequent Releases

In February 2001, 17 software developers met in a ski resort in Utah, USA, to discuss software development methodologies and find common ground and a better way forward. What came out of their time together was the Agile manifesto—a document that has dramatically changed the way people develop software and that still has a huge lasting impact today, over two decades later.

The principles of the Agile manifesto very much align with and complement the ways of working that enable CI/CD. The very first of the 12 principles of the Agile manifesto, for example, reads: "Our highest priority is to satisfy the customer through early and continuous delivery of valuable software" ("Agile Manifesto," 2001). One of the core tenets of Agile is that you deliver working software to your customer as early and often as possible, get customer feedback on your working software, and pivot according to that feedback. Continuous deployment of your software is the very best and easiest way to do that. With CI/CD, your software is always in a working, deliverable state and so can always be put in front of a customer or an end user in order to gather their feedback.

High-performing development teams deploy their software to production, on demand, as soon as a piece of working code has been delivered, many times a day. If every time you can deploy your application, you do deploy your application, then it also allows you to get customer feedback at every possible opportunity too.

We also already know from the DORA State of DevOps reports over the years that small and frequent releases reduce the chance for errors, save teams time, lead to better-quality software, and ultimately lead to more successful and more profitable organizations.

Small Releases

Small releases are beneficial for the above reasons and many more. As has just been mentioned, if you release small changes often, you can get customer feedback often. But they're also good because they make deployments much easier and much more reliable. When you have five changes in a testing cycle and the tests fail, how can you be sure which ticket is the problem? Which developer has the context to fix said problem? What about if the tests pass but your monitors trigger in production? How will you know which change is causing the issue?

Small releases allow you to pinpoint exactly where issues originate. If you release every change to production every time it's possible for you to do so, you know which change caused the issue—the last one. This precision in identifying and addressing issues is a game-changer. If something happens in production, you can pinpoint exactly which change caused it, and you know exactly which change to roll back to fix it.

Developers also can, and should, own their own change through to production this way. There is no need to throw a change over the fence to a test team or a release manager. Given it's only that developer's change going out, if something goes wrong in production, that developer should have all the necessary context to either fix it or roll it back. This is the reason that the best-performing development teams recover from problems within an hour and the worst-performing development teams can take months to recover from issues in production (DORA, 2023).

As the Agile manifesto says: "At regular intervals, the team reflects on how to become more effective, then tunes and adjusts its behaviour accordingly." When you do run into production incidents, make sure you hold postmortems for your team. Put together a timeline of the events, and have a (blame-free) discussion about how you might be able to recover faster next time and what you can add to your deployment pipeline and team processes to make sure similar bugs won't slip through next time.

The concept of small, frequent releases not only aligns with Agile principles but is also essential to a good CI/CD culture. By delivering software in small increments, teams can better manage their workload and ensure that each piece of code is thoroughly tested before reaching the end user. This approach mitigates risks associated with large, infrequent releases, where the volume of changes can make pinpointing issues challenging. It also encourages your team to split their work into discrete deliverable items of work—a fundamental part of the Agile methodology.

Small releases also promote a culture of continuous improvement. Each release is an opportunity to learn and adapt. Teams can gather insights from each deployment, understanding what works well and what doesn't. This iterative process helps foster a more dynamic and responsive development environment, where adjustments are made in real time based on actual feedback. This can be qualitative feedback based on end users' impressions, but also quantitative feedback from logs and monitoring or observations from developers themselves on developer experience, logs and monitoring, or performance.

In practice, implementing small frequent releases requires robust automation and monitoring systems. Automation ensures that each release can be deployed quickly and reliably, without the need for extensive manual intervention. Monitoring systems, on the other hand, provide the necessary visibility into the performance of each release, allowing teams to detect and address issues promptly.

By embracing small, frequent releases, organizations can achieve a higher level of agility and responsiveness. They can quickly adapt to changing market demands, continuously deliver value to their customers, and maintain a competitive edge. The practices outlined in the Agile manifesto, combined with the principles of CI/CD, provide a powerful framework for achieving these goals.

In addition to the operational advantages, small, frequent releases have a really profound impact on team morale and productivity. When developers can see their work go live quickly, it fosters a sense of accomplishment and motivation. This ability to deliver features and fixes so rapidly generally leads to teams that are more engaged with their work, as they can see the direct impact of their efforts on their applications' end users. This heightened engagement might even lead to higher job satisfaction and lower turnover rates of better-quality developers, when compared with organizations where developers barely ever see their changes go live and impact users.

When changes are made and deployed frequently, it does sometimes then require more continuous communication among team members and outside teams. This communication ensures that everyone is aligned on the project goals and aware of the latest developments. It also enables faster resolution of conflicts or misunderstandings as issues can be addressed in real time rather than festering until a major release. The Agile manifesto covers how to handle this communication with its very first value: "*Individuals and interactions over processes and tools.*" Changes shouldn't be scary—and neither should talking to other developers and teams about these changes. Developers can sometimes become comfortable in their own silos! Teams work better when we can break these silos down.

Small releases also support better risk management. By breaking down the development process into smaller, manageable chunks, teams can identify potential issues early and address them before they escalate. This proactive approach to risk management reduces the likelihood of major setbacks and ensures that any problems that do arise are easier to handle. This feedback loop created by frequent releases allows teams to iterate quickly and make data-driven decisions and enhances a team's ability to manage risks effectively. This is the stark opposite from a team who deploy huge releases and who don't release often enough to know where they might have problems and how they might find these problems if they do occur.

It's also important not to overlook the absolute key impact of releasing often—the positive impact on your customer. In today's world, customers expect regular updates and improvements to their software. By delivering small updates frequently, you are able to keep your customers engaged and satisfied. It provides you an opportunity to respond to customer feedback promptly. All of this not only enhances user experience but also builds trust and loyalty, which are crucial for the long-term success of a technology company.

Small, frequent releases are an absolute cornerstone of CI/CD. They enable teams to deliver high-quality software quickly, gather valuable feedback, and continuously iterate on their product and processes. By integrating these practices into their development workflows, organizations can ensure that they remain agile, responsive, and capable of meeting the needs of their customers. The benefits of this approach extend beyond operational efficiency to include enhanced team morale, better risk management, improved customer satisfaction, and, ultimately, a stronger, more competitive position in the market.

Deployments

It's important that your deployment pipeline is the one and only way to push changes to production. This provides the consistency, reliability, and auditability that continuous deployment requires to work effectively. CD is an abbreviation that has two meanings within the industry, and the way your pipeline actually works will depend on which you want to implement. The majority of teams, particularly if they're building web applications, should be aiming to move toward continuous deployment. It is the process described in this book whereby you integrate, test, deploy, and monitor your changes in an automated way. Your pipeline will trigger on merge and bring your changes straight through to production in an automated way, without any manual human intervention. Continuous delivery is slightly different; it is an approach whereby your team still continuously integrates small changes often and still automates the whole build and delivery process as much as possible to ensure small, frequent, well-tested, low-risk releases. In fact, generally continuous delivery will contain all of the same steps and processes as continuous deployment, except that in the case of continuous delivery, the decision to deploy to production will be triggered manually by a team member. As we mentioned in Chapter 1, this might be better for cases where you can't or don't want to Deployment: support multiple releases or you can't or don't want to deploy to customers too often—perhaps you're creating a mobile or desktop app and don't want to pester people to update too often, or perhaps you have a commercial agreement to support a number of releases of your application and adding another at this time would add too much to the workload of your development teams.

In both continuous deployment and continuous delivery though, your main branch will always be fully tested and in a releasable, deployable state. So how can you create a pipeline that ensures that?

What Does a Good Pipeline Look Like?

With CI/CD, your pipeline should be the one way to get your code through to your production environment. You must avoid workarounds or manual changes to the code or infrastructure that makes up your live environment. This allows for consistency and reliability and allows your pipeline to be the one place where you can define whether or not each of the commits made to your codebase is releasable. Because it is the sole identifier of releasability, it is incredibly important that your pipeline is reliable, efficient, and trustworthy.

There is no way of knowing exactly what steps you'll need in your pipeline, as each application is different, but your pipeline should be both deterministic and idempotent. If you run your pipeline twice, on the same codebase, you should get a completely identical outcome each time. It should do this quickly and efficiently. The goal of this process is to be able to take every commit every developer on the team makes and, many times a day, take these commits all the way through to production (or, at the very least, to publishing a releasable artifact).

To ascertain the exact steps you need in your own pipeline, you can follow the principles of Agile and CI/CD and improve your pipeline iteratively as you gather feedback from your users (developers in this case) and discover extra requirements. There's really no need to design the whole pipeline up front and take a waterfall approach to building it. It is much better to tackle your pipeline in small steps, iteratively, just as you would an application, improving as you progress and learn more.

The main requirement of a good pipeline is testing whether your application is ready to release given its latest change, and so you should be running a comprehensive automated testing suite. These tests should be fast, reliable, and repeatable. Test "flakes" (i.e., occasionally failing tests) reduce confidence in your pipeline and should be fixed as your team's priority, and if you can't fix them, flaky tests should be turned off altogether. Your pipeline should be a reliable indicator of whether or not your application is ready to be released to end users. If your pipeline sometimes fails even when your code is in a releasable state, then your pipeline is not efficient, idempotent, or reliable.

You should also be able to rely on these tests (and the pipeline generally) to fail quickly, so developers can use the pipeline to get quick feedback if their application *isn't* releasable. Each developer will be running this automated process multiple times every day, probably once an hour or more, and so if your pipeline takes an hour to fail (particular if there's nothing wrong with the code and the pipeline just requires a rerun), you could be clocking up hours and hours of wasted time a day across your team. Fast and frequent feedback for developers is absolutely key.

This also means that if you do "block" the pipeline, perhaps by merging a change that fails your acceptance tests, unblocking the pipeline should be priority number one for the whole team. The pipeline should be unblocked in the quickest way possible, which typically means rolling back the last change. You can then discuss why and how the breaking change was merged and whether you could have had better-quality indicators earlier in your process (e.g., when the CI build ran against your branch) to avoid this outcome in the future. This discussion should be blame-free, as a culture of psychological safety is key to the way successful software teams work, but it should still happen in case there are learnings that can be taken and improvements that can be made. Learning from mistakes is key in an agile approach to building any software product, and building pipelines is no different.

So pipelines should provide a reliable, consistent indicator of whether your application is ready to release, and they should do so quickly so that developers can get fast feedback. But they can also be used for lots of other useful things. They can be built to help provide an audit trail of what was released and when, they can be used to give you statistics on lead time or throughput, you can use them to store historical audits of test results (including the outcome of performance tests), they can use integrations with a tool like Jira to automatically move your tickets across the board or reduce toil, they can autogenerate audit trails on your Jira ticket itself so you can see the exact time and date specific changes were deployed, they can automatically alert third-party teams of a new release, and whatever other magically useful steps you can think of. Because your pipeline is the only path to production, you get the benefit of being able to rely on this process to kick off any automated steps you might want, or gather any data you might find useful, on all and every production release. These sorts of steps can help you make evidence-based decisions in the future and can be massively useful for high-performing software teams.

Feature Flags

Feature flagging is another way to enable safe and frequent deployments to production. There are many ways to do this, from simple conditionals to enterprise feature flagging solutions, but the concept is the same—turn off a certain branch of code, or feature, so you can continue to merge and deploy your code even if it isn't yet ready for public consumption. This allows you to continue to practice CI/CD and avoid long-lived messy difficult-to-merge feature branches while still allowing you a way to work on long complicated improvements to your application.

I recently worked on a software project where we didn't utilize feature flags properly and essentially abandoned CI to try and dig ourselves out of a difficult spot. This project was a high-profile project within the organization and was a shared platform used by many teams, which meant lots of feature requests coming into us from different areas and teams across the business. But we had a problem—our frontend framework needed an upgrade that would require large-scale changes across the codebase. The old version of this framework was nearing end of life and going out of support, and to carry on receiving security and maintenance updates, it was imperative we upgraded soon. So what did we do? We lobbied for a code freeze with every one of our stakeholders, opened up a long-lived branch where we could work away on the upgrade, and left our main branch for critical and breakfix code changes. The feature freeze lasted for double the amount of time as it should have, as we fought complicated weekly rebases onto our main branch, maintained tests across two branches, and fixed every bug twice across both branches. And after a while of being past our deadlines, the business became (understandably) impatient, which led to feature requests slowly starting to creep back in and rebases becoming even more difficult. When the code freeze finally lifted, we were met with an intimidatingly long list of feature requests that had been left to build up over the weeks and months of code freeze and a feeling of stress any time the words "rebase" and "merge" were uttered aloud.

How might we have used some of the ideas we've talked about so far to approach this upgrade better? Would it have been more successful to deliver the upgrade to production in small chunks behind feature flags or to have found some way to continuously integrate our long-lived branch into main? I'd argue, yes, it would have. In fact, you really should be avoiding code freezes at all costs. High-performing teams, as a rule, tend to completely avoid "code freeze" or stabilization periods (*Accelerate*, 2018).

Implementing feature flags would have allowed us to integrate our changes incrementally without disrupting the main branch. Feature flags enable developers to merge incomplete features into the main branch by hiding them behind a conditional flag that can be turned on or off. This approach keeps the main branch stable and deployable at all times while still allowing the team to work on long-running features that aren't yet ready to release. If we had used feature flags, we could have gradually integrated the new frontend framework, enabling, testing, and deploying small parts of the upgrade as we progressed. This would have made the process much more manageable and much less error-prone and probably would have kept our stakeholders happier to boot.

This would have allowed us to continuously integrate our changes into our main branch, which would have helped us avoid the painful and error-prone process of long-lived branches and massive rebases full of difficult merge conflicts. Instead of one part of the team working on one branch in isolation, each incremental change could have been merged, tested, and validated against the main branch regularly. This approach ensures that any conflicts are detected early and that the integration process remains smooth throughout. It also allows the team to receive continuous feedback on their changes, making it easier to identify and fix any new issues as they arise.

The absence of feature flags and continuous integration in our project led to several challenges. The code freeze created a bottleneck, halting the flow of new features and improvements. This pause not only delayed the delivery of value to our users but also resulted in a backlog of requests that overwhelmed the team once the freeze was lifted. Additionally, maintaining tests across two branches and fixing bugs twice was a significant drain on resources and morale. It created a stressful environment where the team was constantly firefighting instead of focusing on productive development.

High-performing teams understand the importance of maintaining a steady flow of changes and avoiding disruptions like code freezes. They utilize techniques like feature flagging to keep their main branch deployable at all times, enabling the continuous delivery of user value. By embracing these practices, they can handle complex upgrades and feature development without compromising the stability and reliability of their application.

This experience underscored to me the value of feature flagging and continuous integration in managing large-scale changes. These practices help maintain a stable and deployable main branch, avoid the pitfalls of long-lived branches, and ensure a continuous flow of value to users. Avoiding code freezes and adopting these techniques can significantly enhance the efficiency and effectiveness of software development teams, enabling them to deliver high-quality software quickly and reliably.

41

Own Your Own Changes

It is also fundamental with CI/CD that developers own their own changes through to production. There should rarely be a situation in which a developer makes a change and then gives that change to someone else to deploy (barring annual leave, illness, or absence for any other reason). Developers know their own change, they themselves wrote the tests that check the releasability of that change, and they know the logs and alerts they've added to ensure their code is continuously working in production as expected. Perhaps they need a dashboard to reliably ascertain whether or not traffic is flowing through their code in an expected way—if so, they should have been responsible for the creation of this dashboard (or for modifying a current one) and will be best placed to monitor this dashboard as their release hits users in production.

When developers are responsible for their changes from development to deployment, it fosters a sense of ownership and accountability. This ownership ensures that developers are fully engaged in every stage of the software delivery lifecycle, from coding and testing to deployment and monitoring. By maintaining this continuity, developers can quickly respond to issues that arise post-deployment because they are the ones intimately familiar with the changes they themselves made.

It makes sense, right? The developer making the change has the most context on the code they've changed and the most knowledge of the functionality the user is expected to see—so why should they pass the production release (which is arguably the most important part of the entire software delivery lifecycle) to a release manager or a tester? The developer taking this direct responsibility eliminates any unnecessary handoff, which could otherwise introduce delays and miscommunications, and the experience that that extra exposure to real production issues gives them may even lead to developers becoming naturally more predisposed to writing higher-quality code and better, more comprehensive automated tests. Particularly as they'll be the one having to deal with any issues if they do occur! A better working experience on how to avoid certain issues occurring and extra exposure to real incidents in prod can only help lead to developers who know how to write better code in the future.

Involving developers in the deployment process also encourages better logging and monitoring practices. Developers are best placed to ensure that sufficient logs and alerts are in place to track the behavior of their change in production. This proactive approach helps in quickly identifying and diagnosing problems, reducing downtime, and improving the reliability of the application. By being involved in monitoring, developers can gather valuable insights into how their code performs under real-world conditions, leading to better optimizations and enhancements, as well as a better-rounded, more experienced software engineer.

Developers taking on this kind of work is one of the core principles of DevOps, where the goal is to break down silos between development and operations teams. By owning their changes through to production, developers naturally adopt a more holistic view of the software lifecycle. They consider not just the functional aspects of their code but also its operational impact, such as performance, scalability, and security. This integrated perspective is crucial for building high-performing teams that deliver robust, high-quality applications.

When developers handle the entire process, from writing code to deploying it, it also simplifies troubleshooting and debugging. If an issue does arise (which at some point it will), the developer who wrote the code and created the tests is the best person to understand what might have gone wrong. They can quickly investigate the logs and metrics they set up, identify the root cause, and implement a fix. This streamlined approach reduces the time to resolution and minimizes the impact on users.

Ultimately, ensuring that developers own their changes through to production enhances the quality and reliability of your software. It promotes a culture of accountability, encourages best practices in logging and monitoring, and aligns with the DevOps philosophy of breaking down silos.

This integrated perspective is crucial to a DevOps culture. By eliminating handoffs and empowering developers to see their changes through to deployment, organizations can achieve faster, more reliable, and more efficient software delivery.

In fact, really it's fundamental with CI/CD that developers own their own changes. It should simply not be the regular working process that a developer makes a change and then gives that change to someone else in the team to deploy. Perhaps they need a dashboard to reliably ascertain whether or not traffic is flowing through their code in an expected way—if so, they

Additionally, giving developers control over the deployment process empowers them to make continuous improvements. They can experiment with deployment strategies, optimize performance, and iterate on their logging, monitoring, and alerting setups. This continuous improvement cycle leads to a more resilient and efficient software delivery process and better overall observability of your product.

Ultimately, ensuring that developers own their changes through to production enhances the quality and reliability of the software. It promotes a culture of accountability, encourages best practices in logging and monitoring, and aligns with a good DevOps culture and helps organizations achieve faster, more reliable, and more efficient software delivery.

Deployment Strategies

With continuous deployment, your team might feasibly now be deploying to production between 10 and 20 times a day—perhaps more. This frequent deployment capability signifies that your development process has reached a level of maturity and efficiency where rapid iterations and constant improvements have now become possible. You've likely created comprehensive dashboards, integrated alerts, and added detailed logs to meticulously monitor the health and performance of your application in your production environment. These tools provide immediate visibility into the system, allowing you to quickly identify and address issues as soon as they arise. Your robust suite of automated tests ensures that both new and old functionality is always operating correctly, validating that each change meets the required standards of the team before it goes live. Performance tests might further confirm that your application is ready and able to handle the expected load and continue to operate efficiently under various traffic conditions.

So now that you've established this solid but dreamy foundation, what's next? Is it simply time to throw your code into the hands of your production users and hope for the best? While the temptation to leverage this newfound agility is strong, it's also crucial to consider the potential pitfalls associated with very frequent deployments. Downtime during deployment is one major concern. Even a brief period of unavailability can significantly impact user experience, leading to dissatisfaction and potential loss of business. Minimizing or eliminating downtime is essential, especially if you're going to be deploying to users tens of times a day.

And what happens if something does go wrong during a deployment? Despite thorough testing, unforeseen issues can and definitely will still occur, necessitating a quick rollback to the previous stable state. Handling such scenarios gracefully is critical to maintaining user trust and ensuring the reliability of your application.

To address all of these concerns, it's essential to implement smarter deployment strategies that ensure your users can continue to receive a consistent and reliable experience. There are strategies you can follow that will not only help mitigate the risk of downtime but maybe even provide a mechanism for quickly and automatically rolling back changes if any issues are indeed detected.

Blue/Green Deployments

Blue/green deployments can be used to help avoid risk and allow for zero-downtime deployments by running two identical production environments: one designated as "blue" and the other as "green." At any given time only one of these environments will actively be serving traffic to production users, with the other environment either waiting on standby or provisioned directly beforehand in the cloud, to be used during deployments and helping you provide seamless zero-downtime deployments to users.

When you decide to deploy a new version of your application, this deployment process begins with the setup of your green environment. You will want this green environment to exactly mirror the blue environment (i.e., your current live production environment). This will involve copying the current state, configuration, and data to the green environment to ensure it is an exact replica of the blue environment. If you are working in the cloud, this step may also include the complete provisioning of your green environment, as you might want to tear down your "spare" environment when it isn't in use to reduce your bills. Once this setup is complete, you are ready to deploy the new version of your application to the green environment. This part would be done as normal, as if you were deploying to your usual server.

Before routing any live traffic to the green environment, it is then crucial to thoroughly test the new deployment. This testing can be done manually by your QA team or, preferably, through automated tests that ensure the new code meets all necessary standards and performs as expected. Automated testing is often more efficient and reliable, providing comprehensive coverage quickly and consistently, and means that you don't have to stop your deployments to wait for a manual effort from the team.

After you are satisfied with the testing results and confident that the green environment is stable, you can switch the live traffic from the blue environment to the green environment. This switch can be done via your load balancer, reverse proxy, CDN (Cloudflare, CloudFront, etc.), or whichever system can be configured to redirect traffic to the green environment with minimal downtime. This transition should be instantaneous, allowing users to continue using the application without any noticeable interruption. Your newly tested green environment will now be serving users.

Once the green environment is live, continuous monitoring is essential to ensure everything continues to function correctly. This involves keeping an eye on performance metrics, error logs, and user feedback to detect any issues early. If problems arise that cannot be quickly resolved, the blue/green deployment strategy allows for a swift rollback. By reconfiguring your load balancer to redirect traffic back to the blue environment, you can mitigate the impact of a failed or faulty deployment almost instantly.

By having this ability to really easily roll back in an instant if you encounter any issues, you have the ability to ensure that users experience a seamless transition between versions, significantly reducing the risk of disruptions. It means you can also almost guarantee zero downtime, even if something does go wrong.

Blue/green deployments are not without challenges, of course. Managing data synchronization between two active production environments can be complex. It is crucial to ensure that both environments are writing to and reading from the correct data sources. This often involves setting up sophisticated database replication, message queue configuration, and synchronization mechanisms to prevent data inconsistencies.

Maintaining two fully integrated production environments can also be costly. This approach requires additional resources and infrastructure, which can increase your infrastructure bills and add complexity to your pipeline. It is important to weigh these costs against the benefits you're getting from deploying your specific application in this way.

Another challenge is the risk associated with switching live traffic all at once. Despite thorough testing, some issues might only become apparent under real-world conditions. So robust monitoring and quick rollback capabilities are essential.

Despite this complexity, blue/green deployments provide a really powerful mechanism for achieving zero downtime and easy rollbacks during deployments. With careful planning and execution, blue/green deployments can significantly enhance the reliability and user experience of your application.

The main disadvantage deploying applications—particularly complex applications—in this way is that you require two fully integrated and working production environments; this can be really rather costly, both in terms of your cloud provider bill and in terms of complexity.

Figure 2-2 illustrates the three stages of a blue/green deployment.

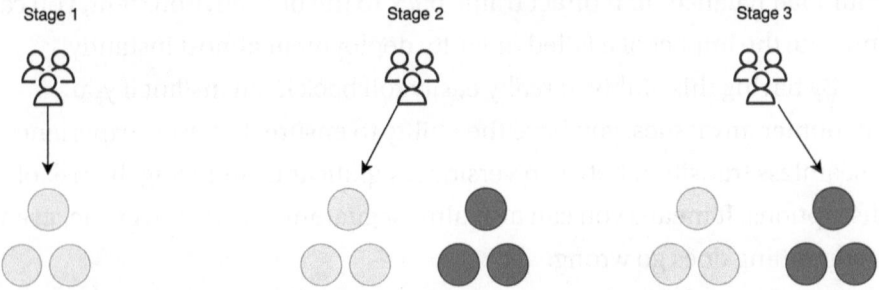

Figure 2-2. *A blue/green deployment*

Rolling Deployments

A rolling deployment involves releasing your application in small incremental batches to each of your servers. The idea is to gradually replace the old version of your application with your new application one "batch" at a time, without any downtime. This approach ensures that at no point is the entire system taken offline, thus maintaining continuous availability for users.

Similar to a blue/green deployment, you will deploy to some of your servers, monitor those servers for problems, and then continue with more until you've completely replaced the old application. The difference is that, when each server is healthy, it will be placed in the pool of live production servers and start serving traffic to real users immediately.

This incremental process allows for close monitoring and the ability to pause or roll back the deployment if issues are detected. If, at any time, there are issues, you can roll back just the deployed servers to the old version of your application. This can also be done seamlessly, ensuring minimal disruption. A tool like Kubernetes allows for rolling deployments out of the box, where you fully deploy and check the health and liveness of one replica before then moving on to the next and the next, until all replicas in the replica set are on the new version of your application. Kubernetes can fully manage this rolling deployment process itself, ensuring that each replica is running correctly before proceeding to the next one.

Rolling deployments help work around some of the bigger disadvantages of blue/green deployments by negating the need for two full production environments. This approach reduces the overhead, complexity, and cost associated with maintaining parallel environments. Rolling deployments are also better for managing some of the risk associated with a "big bang" switchover of traffic at the end of your deployment. By updating a few instances at a time, rolling deployments ensure a more controlled and gradual transition to production, which can help mitigate any potential risks and issues.

Rolling deployments do come with their own level of complexity though. Any consumers of your service will have to support both the old and new versions of your application, as both could be serving traffic in production at the same time. This requires careful planning and coordination to ensure compatibility and consistent behavior across versions. It may involve additional testing and validation to confirm that both versions can coexist without causing issues. This might also cause unexpected or inconsistent experiences for your users during any ongoing deployment process. Users might experience slight differences in behavior depending on which version they interact with or which server has happened to serve their request, leading to potential confusion or inconsistency.

Handling database migrations can also be particularly challenging in a rolling deployment scenario. If the new version of your application requires changes to the database schema, you must ensure that these changes are backward compatible with the old version. This often involves implementing complex migration strategies, such as versioned migrations or feature flags, to manage the transition smoothly.

Despite these challenges, rolling deployments offer significant benefits in terms of reducing downtime and mitigating risk. By carefully managing the deployment process and ensuring thorough testing and monitoring, you can achieve a smooth and efficient rollout of new application versions. This approach allows for continuous delivery and rapid iteration, enabling your development team to respond quickly to user feedback and changing requirements.

While they do introduce some complexity, particularly in terms of managing compatibility and user experience, the benefits of reduced downtime and more controlled deployment could make them an attractive option for many organizations. By leveraging tools like Kubernetes and implementing best practices for deployment and monitoring, you can effectively manage the challenges and reap the rewards of rolling deployments.

Figure 2-3 illustrates the three stages of a rolling deployment.

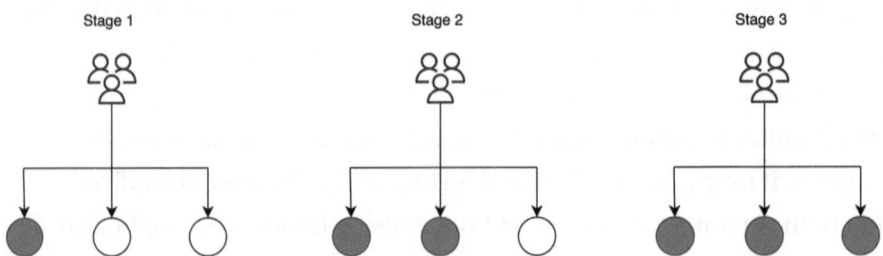

Figure 2-3. *A rolling deployment*

Canary Deployments

Canary deployments[1] involve gradually rolling out the new version of your application to a specific percentage of users before rolling out a full release. This deployment strategy is designed to mitigate risk by allowing you to observe how the new version performs under actual production conditions, with real production users, before committing to a full-scale rollout. This incremental approach helps identify potential issues early on, reducing the likelihood of widespread user impact if a problem does arise during deployment.

The fundamental advantage of canary deployments is the ability to monitor and assess the new release in a controlled manner but under real-life conditions in your real production environment. By exposing only a small subset of users to the update initially, you can gather critical performance data, error data, and user feedback. This early insight can be absolutely invaluable, as it enables you to catch and address real customer-impacting issues that might not be evident in your testing environments during your normal testing cycle. Real-world usage can uncover bugs, performance bottlenecks, and other problems that your automated tests might easily miss.

Implementing canary deployments does require robust and reliable monitoring and alerting systems though. It's crucial to have comprehensive observability in place to track key metrics and detect anomalies quickly. Metrics such as error rates, response times, and user engagement levels should be closely monitored to determine the health of your new release. If these metrics indicate problems, you can halt the deployment, investigate the issues, and make necessary corrections before proceeding further or, if needed, rolling back.

---

[1] Named as such because of the phrase "canary in the coalmine"

Effective canary deployments absolutely hinge on the ability to analyze data from these initial stages and make informed decisions. For instance, deploying to 5% of your user base might reveal no significant increase in error logs, suggesting that the release is stable. At this point, you might increase the deployment to 50% of users, monitoring conversion rates and other critical metrics to ensure they remain consistent and healthy. Each stage should provide real, concrete, actionable insights that guide your next steps.

The decision on what percentage of users to include in each deployment stage should be based on what you aim to learn from that stage. For example, starting with a small percentage like 5% might allow you to catch major showstopping bugs without impacting a large number of users. Subsequent stages, such as increasing to 50%, can focus on evaluating performance and user experience more broadly. Each stage should build on the findings of the previous one, ensuring that by the time you reach 100%, the new version has been thoroughly vetted.

You need the data to be able to do this though. There is absolutely no point adding all of these extra complexity and time to your deployment pipeline if you are just going through the motions of your canary deployment process without learning anything at all from your data. High-performing software development teams make data-driven decisions—but to do that, they need data!

One of the other challenges with canary deployments is the potential for user inconsistencies. During the deployment process, some users will be on the new version, while others remain on the old version. Similarly to rolling deployments, this necessitates that your application can support both versions simultaneously without causing confusion or errors. It requires thoughtful planning and possibly adjustments in how you handle data, user sessions, and feature availability.

Canary deployments often involve more complexity in the deployment pipeline. The process must be carefully orchestrated to ensure that each stage is executed correctly and that rollback procedures are in place should problems arise. Automation plays a crucial role here; a well-designed pipeline can automatically progress through the deployment stages based on predefined criteria, such as passing specific health checks and performance benchmarks.

It's also important to consider the feedback loop from users during the canary deployment process. Engaging with users who are part of the initial deployment can provide qualitative insights that complement your quantitative metrics. Users might report issues that aren't immediately apparent through automated monitoring, such as usability concerns or unexpected behavior under specific conditions. But this is not as automated and adds time and inefficiency to your rollout. So, as mentioned, it is massively important to decide how you will measure the success of each stage and what data you want to collect to do so. The effectiveness of this strategy is very much dependent on the data you use to make decisions throughout the deployment.

By leveraging real-world data and user feedback in a controlled manner, you can ensure that each release is completely robust and reliable in a real-world setting before it reaches your entire user base. To achieve the full benefits of this approach, you must invest in strong monitoring, automate your deployment pipeline, and be prepared to iterate based on the insights you gather. This methodical approach not only enhances the stability of your releases but also builds trust with your users by minimizing disruptions and delivering higher-quality software.

Figure 2-4 illustrates the three stages of a canary deployment.

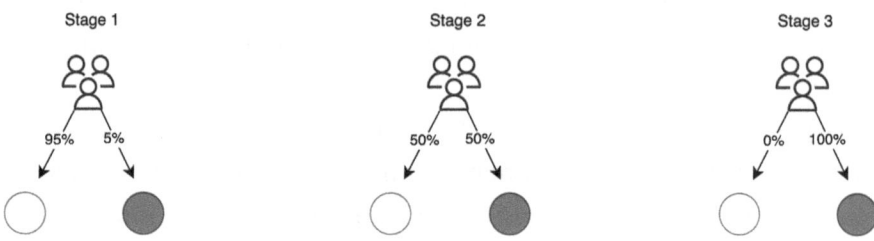

Figure 2-4. *A canary deployment*

Source Control and Branching

Decent source control is vital to CI/CD. It allows you to roll back properly, to code review properly, and to store the history of your application so you can audit what was released and when. Of course, it is rare these days that a professional development team will not have their application in source control (typically Git). The benefits of having robust source control in place extend far beyond merely having a repository for your code though. It isn't just application code you should be keeping in source control. In fact, to leverage the full potential of CI/CD, your source control should encompass all of the elements that make up your application and are integral to your software development lifecycle.

Continuous deployment dictates that we can deploy our whole application in an automated way. If you're hosting in the cloud, this is predicated really on the ability to recreate your environment from scratch with precision, consistency, and idempotency. To do this, we need to be able to provision full environments before building, testing, and deploying our applications to them from scratch or from any broken or half-deployed state your environment might possibly be in. This requires you to be able to provision environments purely from information kept in your repositories being maintained by source control. This means that not only should your application code be in source control, but your infrastructure code should be as well. We should be keeping the same ways of working with regard to our infrastructure code as we do with our application code, which means continuously integrating changes and deploying as often and in as small batches as possible.

Using infrastructure as code (IaC) tooling like Terraform, Pulumi, or CDK to provision your environments from source control allows you to spin up (from fresh) a whole environment to deploy your working software onto. This enables teams to automate the setup of their infrastructure, ensuring that environments are consistent and repeatable. You can also create production-like integrated environments with this approach, allowing you to run automated tests against realistic environments, giving you more confidence in your production deployment. With IaC, every aspect of your infrastructure—from network configurations to service setups—can be defined in code and version controlled, just like your application code.

Being able to spin up a complete environment, including all of your infrastructure and application code, from scratch is massively helpful both in provisioning new environments and in disaster recovery scenarios. For instance, if a critical failure occurs, you can redeploy a fully functional environment quickly and reliably. This capability significantly reduces downtime and ensures business continuity.

By maintaining infrastructure as code, you ensure that your environments are always in a state that can be recreated accurately, avoiding the drift that can occur with manual changes. You enforce consistency, reduce the risk of human error, and make it easier to troubleshoot issues since the configuration is documented and versioned in your source control, with a full audit of the history of your environments. Automation of your environment setup and teardown not only allows you to accelerate your development cycles but also enables you to easily scale your infrastructure, adapting to varying traffic levels and demands on load with ease. Integrating IaC into your CI/CD pipeline is not just a best practice but a necessity for achieving true agility and reliability in modern software development. Declaring your whole estate in code and avoiding any "snowflake" manual changes in your cloud service control panel helps you audit changes, respects the pipeline as the only path to production, and helps keep your whole estate more maintainable.

Trunk-Based Development

Trunk-based development is a practice whereby, instead of working on long-lived feature branches that may last weeks or months, developers write code in small, atomic commits and push either straight to the main branch or merge their code into main (or trunk) one or many times a day. This practice requires that development teams and developers know how to divide their work up into nice, small deliverable batches and also requires them to continuously integrate their code into a main branch that is always in a deliverable, working state. In fact, you might think this sounds a lot like continuous integration itself.[2] That's because CI *is* trunk-based development—you are writing code and integrating it continuously into the main codebase—but CI has the added component of a fast automated test suite and pipeline that is there to provide you with a decision as to whether or not the code that's just been merged in to trunk is also ready to be released to production.

Teams that aren't using trunk-based development may be using a more complex method like Gitflow to manage their source code and merge strategy. While Gitflow introduces a nice, well-thought-out workflow with multiple branches for feature development, release preparation, and hotfixes, it also creates significant overhead and complexity. Managing multiple long-lived branches increases the risk of merge conflicts and the likelihood of integration issues.

Figure 2-5 illustrates the complexity that can occur in your repository when following the Gitflow workflow.

---

[2] An opinion shared by Martin Fowler who asserts that CI and trunk-based development are synonymous—https://martinfowler.com/articles/continuousIntegration.html#trunk-based

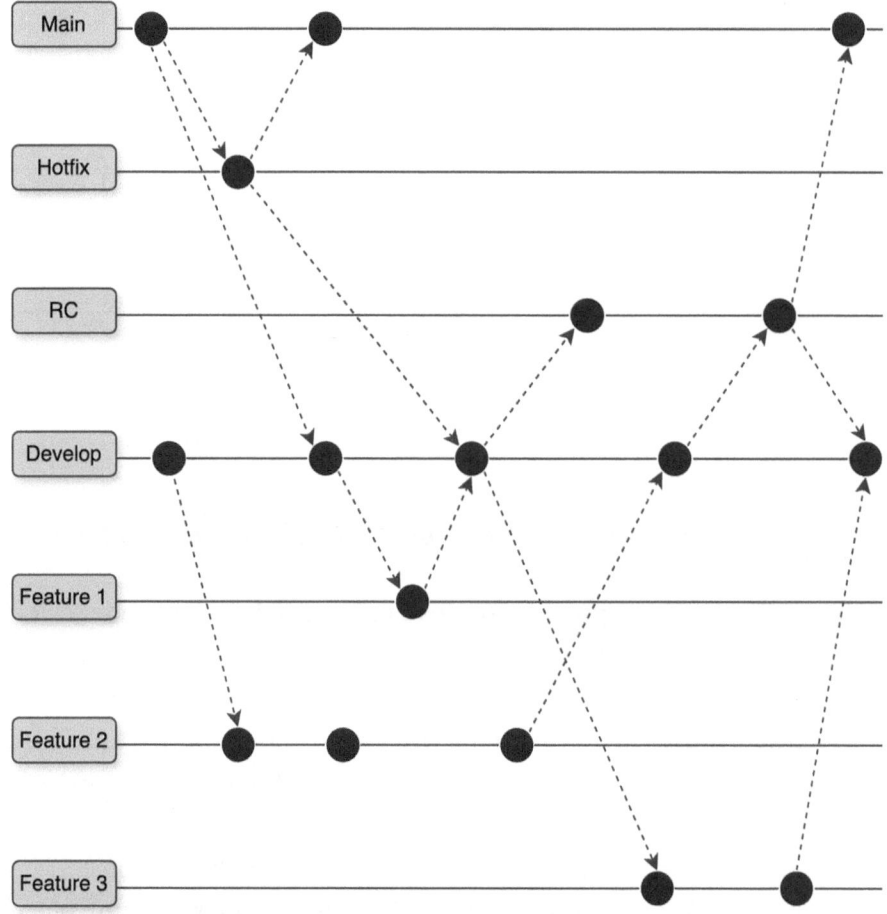

Figure 2-5. *An example of a Gitflow workflow*

Trunk-based development massively simplifies the process by reducing the number of branches and promoting frequent integration. This approach minimizes the potential for nasty merge conflicts and ensures that the main branch remains in a deployable state at all times.

Figure 2-6 is an example of a cleaner workflow with trunk-based development in place.

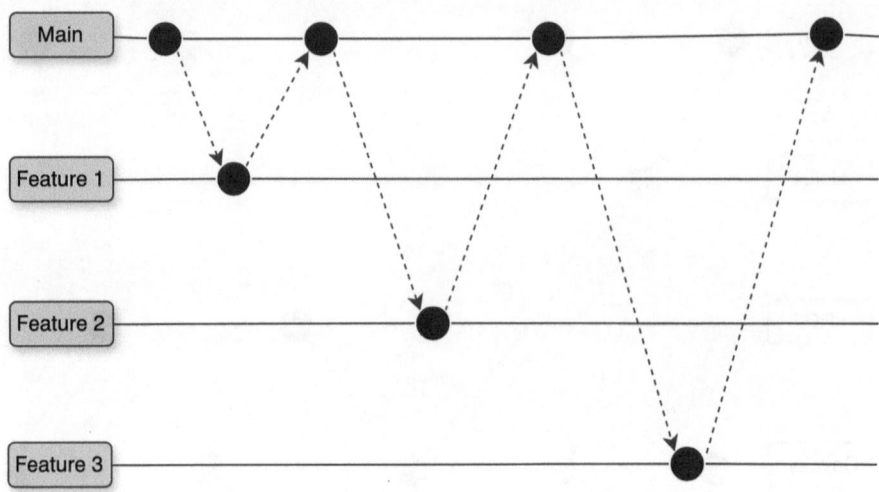

Figure 2-6. *An example of a trunk-based development workflow*

Trunk-based development requires a fast and lightweight code review system. Pairing or mob programming can be the ultimate lightweight way to get multiple developers' eyes on the code, by allowing code to be reviewed synchronously, as it's being written. Generally, both trunk-based development and CI work much better if code can be reviewed as synchronously as possible.

Some development teams make the mistake—with the best of intentions—of taking the complete opposite approach in the pursuit of quality. They might implement an asynchronous, rigorous code review process, in the form of change review boards or specific senior codeowners who must approve every change. This is counterproductive. DORA statistics prove that change management boards are "negatively correlated with tempo and stability" (*Accelerate*, 2018) and that high-performing teams are able to make (even large-scale) changes to their system and complete all of their work without permission from, or even having to communicate to, colleagues outside of their immediate team (*Accelerate*, 2018).

The same report also found that high-performing development teams are more likely to have "fewer than three active branches at any time," branches with "very short lifetimes (less than a day) before being merged into trunk," and zero periods of code freeze (*Accelerate*, 2018). This proves that successful development teams are more likely to be using trunk-based development, as well as being generally brave and proactive about making big innovative changes to their codebases.

Implementing trunk-based development offers a number of key advantages. Firstly, it simplifies the process of integrating new code, reducing the potential for merge conflicts and making it easier to maintain a stable main branch. This in turn promotes frequent integration, ensuring that the codebase remains in a consistently deployable state. Developers are encouraged to commit their changes often, which helps in identifying and resolving integration issues early.

Trunk-based development also enhances collaboration among your team members. By working on a shared main branch, developers are more aware of each other's changes and can collaborate and work with each other more effectively. Just as with CI/CD, this helps foster a culture of collective code ownership, where everyone on the team feels responsible for the quality and stability of the codebase. It facilitates faster feedback as well, as code changes are being reviewed and integrated quickly.

It can also indirectly help to reduce technical debt. Long-lived branches can accumulate changes that diverge significantly from the main branch, making integration cumbersome and error-prone. Trunk-based development mitigates this risk by encouraging small, incremental changes that are merged continuously, in small batches. This approach aligns with the principles of Agile and DevOps and promotes a more iterative and incremental development process.

Trunk-based development also enables faster release cycles for your team. With a stable main branch that is always in a deployable state, teams can release their newly built features and updates much more frequently. This ability to continuously deploy code helps deliver value to customers quickly and can act as a competitive advantage for a technology organization.

On the other hand, successful implementation of trunk-based development does of course require a cultural shift for a lot of development teams, just as CI does. Developers need to adopt a mindset of frequent, small commits and embrace practices like test-driven development (TDD), pair programming, and continuous integration. The team must invest in robust automation and tooling. Automated tests, CI pipelines, and effective code review processes are all essential to maintaining the quality and stability of the codebase while still moving and merging code quickly.

Trunk-based development is a powerful practice that aligns very closely with the principles of CI/CD. By adopting trunk-based development, development teams can maintain a stable and deployable main branch, reduce technical debt, and deliver value to their customers more efficiently. They will be within touching distance of continuous integration. Just some automated tooling and a strong pipeline away! The practices outlined in the Agile manifesto and supported by DORA research provide a solid foundation for proving the merits of and implementing trunk-based development, and therefore continuous integration, successfully.

Key Takeaways

- **CI/CD Foundations:** Transitioning to CI/CD requires a strong foundation, including a reliable automated test suite and the right cultural shift toward frequent, small commits. Both continuous integration (CI) and continuous deployment (CD) rely heavily on automation, testing, and consistent, small changes.

- **Testing:** Automated testing is crucial for CI/CD. It ensures that every change is validated before moving to production, with a strong emphasis on unit tests, integration tests, and UI tests following the testing pyramid model. Manual testing is still a useful tool, but only for specific use cases.

- **Test-Driven Development (TDD):** TDD is essential for creating reliable, modular, and maintainable code. It helps developers write tests before the code, which leads to better design, fewer bugs, and easier refactoring.

- **Small, Frequent Releases:** CI/CD promotes small, frequent releases, enabling faster feedback loops, reducing the risk of errors, and allowing teams to react quickly to customer feedback.

- **Deployment Strategies:** Strategies such as blue/green deployments, rolling deployments, and canary deployments might be able to help ensure smooth, zero-downtime deployments while minimizing risks.

- **Feature Flags:** Using feature flags allows teams to deploy new features incrementally and safely, even if they are not yet ready for full production use.

- **Source Control and Branching:** Proper use of source control, particularly trunk-based development, is vital for successful CI/CD. It minimizes complexity, reduces merge conflicts, and keeps the main branch always in a deployable state.

- **Developer Ownership:** CI/CD practices emphasize
  that developers should own their changes all the way
  through to production. This accountability leads to
  better-quality code, faster resolution of issues, and a
  more efficient development process.

CI/CD is not just about changes to your technical estate. In the next
chapter, we will discuss the cultural and organizational changes that are
needed to make CI/CD a success.

CHAPTER 3

Cultural Shifts

Any technical transformation in an organization requires real cultural change to complement it, and a move toward better CI/CD practices is definitely no exception. So much of CI/CD is about your mental approach to deploying software, your appetite for perceived risk, and the autonomy and confidence your development teams have in their area of the technical estate.

While traditional waterfall development teams are often characterized by silos and functional separation with an emphasis on individual performance, this type of culture is not conducive to CI/CD adoption. The successful adoption of CI/CD requires collaboration, cross-functional teams, agile development methodologies, and an emphasis on team performance, collaboration, and continuous improvement.

So many development teams avoid CI or CD because they and their team are used to operating within a rigid organizational culture, and they either fear changing their approach, don't know how to, or feel they aren't able to. To adopt these practices successfully, teams need to feel empowered to change and manage their own processes and to reflect on issues and potential changes to the process as they go.

When the Build Breaks, Fix It!

When you're working in a project utilizing continuous deployment, your path to production is of paramount importance. This path, or pipeline, is a critical element that every developer on your team utilizes multiple times

© Tommy Clark 2025
T. Clark, *CI/CD Unleashed*, Apress Pocket Guides,
https://doi.org/10.1007/979-8-8688-1209-5_3

a day to deliver code. Until code has passed through this pipeline, the work is not yet considered complete. So the pipeline needs to be efficient, reliable, and stable to avoid wasting the time of your software development teams (and, therefore, your organization's money).

The importance of the stability of your build pipeline cannot be overstated. An unstable pipeline can cause delays, create bottlenecks, and lead to frustration among your development team and your stakeholders. Ensuring a stable and efficient pipeline is absolutely crucial for maintaining productivity and keeping things ticking over smoothly.

When a build breaks or gets stuck or when a bug is discovered in your deployment or build code or even when an issue is discovered in your automated tests, it should trigger an immediate response. The priority level of these issues should be set to P1, meaning it's the top priority for the entire team, and it should be all hands on deck to fix it. The reasoning behind this is straightforward: no work is considered done until it is in production and being used by real users. The build pipeline is the only pathway to move work from development into production, making its integrity and functionality essential.

Immediate Response to Pipeline Issues

To successfully implement continuous deployment, you need to establish a culture where pipeline issues are addressed immediately. The key actions to ensure this are

- **Quick Detection and Alerting:** Implement robust monitoring and alerting systems to quickly detect when the build breaks. This should include automated notifications to alert the relevant team members as soon as an issue is identified.

- **Dedicated Response Team:** At first, you may wish to designate a response team or a rotation system where specific team members are on call to handle build issues. This ensures that there is always someone ready to address and resolve pipeline problems without delay. Eventually this should be embedded into the culture of the whole team, and you shouldn't need designated colleagues to look at it.

- **Collaborative Fixes:** Foster a collaborative environment where fixing build issues is seen as a team responsibility. Encourage team members to assist each other and share knowledge to resolve issues swiftly.

Steps to Stabilize Your Build Pipeline

Ensuring the stability of your build pipeline also involves several proactive steps:

- **Regular Maintenance:** Schedule regular maintenance and updates for your build scripts in order to keep them in optimal condition. This includes updating dependencies, clearing caches, and optimizing for performance.

- **Continuous Monitoring:** Implement continuous monitoring tools to track the performance and stability of your build pipeline. Analyze metrics and logs to identify patterns and potential areas of improvement.

Creating a Culture of Immediate Action

Building a culture where pipeline issues are addressed immediately requires clear communication and shared responsibility. Some strategies to embed this culture in your team might be

- **Training and Awareness:** Conduct regular training sessions to ensure all team members understand the importance of a stable build pipeline and their role in maintaining it.

- **Clear Protocols:** Establish clear protocols for handling build issues, including escalation procedures and communication channels. Ensure everyone knows the steps to take when an issue arises and who is designated to take those steps. Ensure everyone knows that maintaining the build is a shared problem.

- **Post-incident Reviews:** Conduct post-incident reviews to analyze what went wrong and how it can be prevented in the future. Use these reviews as learning opportunities to improve your processes and tools, rather than an opportunity to find and place blame.

In a continuous deployment environment, the build pipeline is the absolute lifeline of your development process. Its stability and efficiency directly impact the productivity and success of your software development teams in hitting your organizational goals. By prioritizing the resolution of build issues, fostering a collaborative and responsive culture, and implementing proactive measures to stabilize your pipeline, you can ensure your path to production stays smooth and reliable.

Remember: no work can be "done" until it is in production being used by real users, and this pipeline is the only way to get work through to production. Make sure when the build breaks, the team knows that it's priority to fix it.

Deliver Iteratively

You cannot have continuous deployment without an Agile methodology, and small, frequent releases are absolutely key to that. CI/CD dictates that you deliver your code in small chunks, which can be easily tested, integrated, deployed, monitored, and rolled back as needed.

Delivering in these small chunks also allows you to pivot in an agile way to either a change in customer needs or any actionable feedback you might receive when showcasing your usable and working software milestones. This iterative approach means you're not only enhancing the efficiency of your deployment pipeline but also significantly improving the adaptability of your team.

The Importance of Small, Frequent Releases

Delivering code in small chunks is a key part of both Agile methodology and CI/CD. This approach ensures that changes are incremental, manageable, and less risky. Each small release allows for thorough testing and quick integration, making it easier to identify and resolve issues early in the development cycle. This proactive problem-solving reduces the chances of major disruptions and enhances the overall stability of your software.

By delivering in small increments, teams can respond more effectively to changing customer needs and feedback. This agile responsiveness is crucial to success in the software industry, particularly when customer expectations can change rapidly. Small, frequent releases provide a constant flow of improvements and new features, keeping your software relevant and competitive. It also allows you to really keep on top of what's being released at any one time, making monitoring and rollbacks much easier.

Planning and Refining Work into Smaller Chunks

The practice of delivering small chunks of work requires a conscious cultural shift within the team. It's not just about breaking down tasks but adopting a mindset that prioritizes simplicity and efficiency. Teams need to ask themselves, "How can we make this ticket smaller?" This question should be a fundamental part of the planning and refining process.

In traditional development environments that rely on big bang releases, the tendency is to bundle numerous changes together, leading to complex and often problematic deployments. This "while we're here ..." approach can actually cause significant delays, comes with more risk, and can increase the risk of conflicts when integrating with the main codebase. CI/CD encourages a more disciplined and incremental approach, ensuring that each piece of work is a discrete, manageable unit that can be easily integrated into your main branch and quickly rolled back if something goes wrong.

Implementing Cultural Change

Adopting this iterative approach is not without its challenges. Cultural habits, especially those ingrained in traditional development teams, can be tough to change. However, for CI/CD to be effective, it is essential that teams embrace the practice of delivering small, discrete chunks of work. Here are some strategies to foster this cultural shift:

- **Address Concerns:** Engage with team members to understand their concerns and reservations about the new approach. Provide clear explanations and address any misconceptions.

- **Provide Support:** Offer support and resources to help team members adapt to the new practices. This could include mentoring, additional training, and access to Agile coaches.

- **Use Tools and Metrics:** Leverage project management tools that support Agile practices like user story mapping and task boards. Use the metrics from these tools to track the size and flow of tasks through the pipeline. Jira, for example, has built-in tooling to enable this tracking.

- **Showcase Benefits:** Regularly showcase the benefits of iterative delivery through metrics and success stories. Demonstrating the tangible improvements in productivity, quality, and customer satisfaction can help build buy-in.

- **Create a Safe Environment:** Encourage an environment where experimentation and learning are valued. Allow team members to make mistakes and learn from them without fear of blame or retribution. You won't always slice tickets correctly—some will be too small and some will be too big. Learn from your mistakes and improve for next time.

Delivering iteratively is a fundamental aspect of CI/CD and Agile methodologies. It enables teams to respond quickly to changes, deliver high-quality software, and continuously improve their processes. By embracing the practice of delivering small, manageable chunks of work, teams can achieve greater efficiency, stability, and adaptability. While the cultural shift required may be challenging, the long-term benefits to the development process and overall organizational success are well worth the effort.

Any cultural habit in any organization or team is tough to change, and this is no different, but CI/CD will work best if tickets are small, discrete chunks of work that can flow through the entire board quickly.

Keep Things Blameless

When deployments do go wrong—and they of course will at some point—blaming individuals is entirely pointless. Blaming individuals is the easy way out, allowing you as a team not to make any changes or harden any of your processes. Depending on the culture of your team, some team members may feel it is the noble thing for them to do to fall on their sword and accept the blame for a mistake which cost the company money or reputational damage. Don't allow them to do this. Do the difficult work instead and consider what you can all do differently in terms of process.

Postmortems (or root cause analyses, or retrospectives, or whatever you might want to call them) are a great way to do this. Gather your team and talk through:

1. **What happened?**
    Create a timeline together of the events that led to your incident and anything that happened in the aftermath of said incident. Include any notable and relevant decisions, interactions, failures, errors, and consequences, and include actions taken both by people inside the team and outside the team and any external factors that either contributed to the incident happening or exacerbated the impact of the incident.
    This should give your team a great shared understanding of what happened, the factors that played a part, and make the rest of the exercise easier.

2. **How might we stop this from happening again?**
    Get the team to brainstorm methods for prevention. Everyone can grab a pack of Post-It notes, all shout out ideas, have a robust discussion, or however else

your team likes to communicate. Produce a number of plans and ideas that would have prevented or reduced the likelihood of this issue happening.

3. **How could we have reduced the blast radius?**
Repeat the above exercise, but this time focusing on how you could have reduced the blast radius of your change. When you move quickly as a development team, you might make mistakes. It's important when you do that those mistakes are as contained and managed as they possibly can be. One back-office microservice deploying to production when it shouldn't, shouldn't take down the whole website!

4. **Prioritize and create actions**
After you've created your lists, prioritize (dot vote, discuss—again, whatever is best for your team's communication style), and create real actions that your team can progress. This is the most important part of the session! Discussing these issues is great, but creating and carrying out actions is the main way your team processes will improve.

Avoid calling out team members by name during each of these actions. All you'll do by calling people out is affect the team's psychological safety. It is also the "easy way out." The whole team is responsible for creating a hardy, stable, and reliable path to production, so blaming one person for getting something wrong is letting the whole team off when really they should be studying the processes and considering how they might improve to mitigate or lessen the impact and likelihood of the inevitable cases of human error that will occur again in the future.

Limit Your WIP

Limiting work in progress (WIP) is a great way to get better at continuous integration and deployment. High-performing teams deliver software quicker, more often, and at a faster pace, and limiting your WIP allows you to do all of the above.

The culture within a team plays a critical role in determining its success. A toxic culture, where individual developers seek personal glory, can severely hinder productivity and team cohesion.

In development teams with a negative culture, developers may be tempted to compete for personal recognition and prioritize their individual achievements over the collective success of the team. This competition may be measured by the number of tickets each developer completes or the amount of the knowledge on the system they can hold in their heads, leading to a fragmented team and a difficult environment. The focus shifts from delivering high-quality work to merely increasing the quantity of work done and amount of knowledge collected, which can result in rushed or subpar outputs.

Trunk-based development and CI/CD methodologies are instead built on principles of collaboration and continuous improvement. Trunk-based development emphasizes the use of short-lived branches that are frequently merged into the main branch. This approach reduces the risk of integration conflicts and ensures that the codebase remains stable and deployable. Teams must collaborate when they are merging into each other's code multiple times a day and deploying the results of that to production.

One symptom of the kind of competitive culture that's incompatible with CI/CD, where developers are driven by personal accolades, is an excessive amount of work in progress. When developers are focused on starting new tasks to showcase their productivity, they neglect the importance of completing and integrating their team's current work. This results in long-lived branches, significant merge conflicts, and delays in deployment. The pipeline becomes congested as team members are perpetually stuck, struggling to reconcile their changes with those of their peers and colleagues and perhaps uncomfortable or unable to ask for help.

In a successful CI/CD culture, development teams limit their work in progress. This requires a fundamental shift in mindset: completing any work currently in progress should take precedence over picking up new tasks. By focusing on finishing existing work, teams can ensure that changes are integrated and deployed more smoothly and efficiently. This involves actively asking if anyone on the team needs help and jumping on to their ticket instead of starting a new one. This approach minimizes bottlenecks, reduces the risk of conflicts, and enhances the overall stability of the codebase.

Creating a culture that prioritizes limited WIP involves buy-in from all team members, including developers, engineering managers, and product owners. Engineering managers must set the tone by promoting practices that encourage collaboration and discourage the initiation of new tasks before completing current ones. Product owners should align their priorities with the team's goals, emphasizing the importance of delivering incremental, well-integrated changes.

To reinforce this culture, teams should establish clear communication channels and create an environment where open dialogue is encouraged. Regular stand-ups, retrospectives, and code reviews provide opportunities for team members to share their progress, address roadblocks, and collectively find solutions.

Several strategies can help teams limit their work in progress. Firstly, adopting WIP limits in task management tools like Jira can prevent developers from taking on too many tasks simultaneously. Implementing metrics that emphasize team performance over individual achievements can shift the focus from personal glory to collective success. And celebrating milestones such as successful deployments and resolved integration challenges as a team can reinforce the importance of teamwork and collaboration.

Investing in tools and practices that facilitate trunk-based development and CI/CD is also crucial. Automated testing, continuous integration pipelines, and feature flags can streamline the integration process and reduce the likelihood of conflicts, making it easier for teams to adhere to WIP limits and deliver their tickets through to production quicker with little input or waiting around required.

Communicate

Effective communication is the backbone of any successful implementation of CI/CD. By creating a culture of collaboration through practices like pair programming, mob programming, and adhering to the Agile principles, development teams can ensure that short-lived branches are integrated as quickly and efficiently as possible. Synchronous pull requests and pair programming can help streamline the workflows of your developers, enabling teams to maintain a clean and up-to-date main branch without waiting around for changes to get through a rigid and long-winded process. The ability to communicate effectively could be all the difference between a chaotic deployment process and a smoothly functioning CI/CD pipeline.

Pair Programming and Mob Programming

Pair programming and mob programming are collaborative techniques that help enhance communication and knowledge sharing among team members. In pair programming, two developers work together on the same piece of code, sharing a single screen and keyboard. One "drives" by sitting at the keyboard and typing, while the other "navigates" by thinking of solutions and suggesting next steps. This practice not only improves code quality but also facilitates continuous feedback and immediate problem-solving.

Mob programming takes this concept further by involving the entire team in a single coding session. With everyone contributing ideas and reviewing the code in real time, the chances of missing critical issues are significantly reduced. These practices embody the Agile principle of "individuals and interactions over processes and tools," emphasizing the importance of human collaboration in achieving technical excellence.

By incorporating pair and mob programming into their workflow, teams can ensure that branches are closed off quickly and integrated continuously into the main branch. The constant interaction among team members helps identify and resolve issues early, leading to smoother and more efficient CI/CD processes and helping tickets move through to done more quickly.

Agile Principles and Communication

The Agile manifesto suggests that teams prioritize individuals and interactions over processes and tools. This principle is particularly relevant to CI/CD implementation, where the focus is on delivering value quickly and efficiently. Agile encourages regular communication through stand-ups, retrospectives, and planning sessions, enabling teams to pivot in response to changing requirements and continuously improve processes.

In an Agile environment, transparency and collaboration are key. Teams that communicate effectively can better manage their workloads, anticipate upcoming challenges, and coordinate efforts to achieve goals. This lightweight people-first approach ensures that short-lived branches are integrated without delay, maintaining the stability and integrity of the main branch. The antithesis of this is change boards, sign-offs, and external reviews, which provide extra process for very little value and provide blockers to your code reaching production.

Synchronous Pull Requests

Synchronous pull requests (PRs) can significantly accelerate workflows by minimizing the time developers spend on their branches while the main branch continues to evolve. In traditional workflows, developers might work on a feature for an extended period, only to find that the main branch has diverged significantly. At this point, the developer will need to carry out a complex and error-prone rebase, fixing all the problems that have come about because of it and then requesting another review of their PR crossing their fingers that they don't encounter the same issue again before they get their sign-off.

By adopting synchronous PRs, teams can review and merge code changes in real time, reducing the risk of conflicts and ensuring that the main branch remains up-to-date. This practice enhances the overall CI/CD process by promoting continuous integration, reducing the likelihood of nasty rebases and getting work in progress through to production quicker. Synchronous PRs require effective communication and collaboration to coordinate reviews, address feedback promptly, and facilitate quick decision-making.

Deploying on a Friday

Throughout the industry of software development, the notion of deploying code on a Friday evening, right before heading off to the pub, is often met with raised eyebrows and apprehensive smiles. This is a controversial point and may, to some, suggest a level of confidence and stability in the development process that few teams feel is achievable. But there is no reason, with a solid and reliable pipeline, to deploy to production on a Friday at 5 PM.

Perhaps this is a slightly tongue-in-cheek recommendation, as team members know more about the particular unique situation that they operate in and can make a much better judgment than me on whether this is something they can realistically achieve without issue. However, the idea behind this controversial point is grounded in an important truth: every software development team should strive for a codebase and deployment pipeline so robust that a Friday evening release is guaranteed to be a complete non-event.

In reality, each software development team does of course operate within a unique context. They are intimately familiar with their codebase, deployment process, organizational appetite for risk, and, ideally, their customers' needs. This intimate knowledge equips teams with the insights necessary to judge the stability and reliability of their deployments. Yet, regardless of these nuances, the ultimate goal should absolutely remain the same: to build a pipeline and codebase that can handle the rigors of a Friday evening deployment with minimal risk and maximum confidence.

Envisioning and striving for a deployment pipeline that supports Friday evening releases fosters a culture of excellence within a development team. It encourages best practices in coding, testing, and monitoring. Moreover, it creates an environment where developers can work with confidence and peace of mind, knowing that their systems are resilient and their processes are reliable.

Deploying code on a Friday evening just before heading to the pub may seem like a whimsical goal, but it represents a deeper aspiration for software development teams. It signifies a commitment to stability, efficiency, thorough testing, effective observability, and seamless rollbacks. By working toward this ideal, teams can ensure that their deployment processes are robust and reliable, ultimately leading to higher-quality software and a more enjoyable working environment. Doesn't that sound like a team you'd want to work in?

Stability and Error Detection

At the heart of a reliable deployment process is stability. The deployment pipeline must be robust enough to catch and flag errors before they reach production. This means having automated tests and checks that ensure the code meets all necessary quality standards. If something does go wrong, the pipeline should fail gracefully, turning red and halting the process to prevent any flawed code from being deployed.

Efficiency in Deployment

Time is of the essence, especially on a Friday evening when everyone is eager to wrap up and start their weekend. An efficient deployment pipeline ensures that the process is quick and smooth. Deployments should be swift enough that developers can wait to see the code through to production without significant delay, ideally before their friends finish ordering that first round of drinks.

Thorough Testing

Confidence in the code being deployed is paramount. This confidence comes from comprehensive testing. Code should be rigorously tested in various environments to ensure it behaves as expected under different conditions. Automated tests should cover a wide range of scenarios, from unit tests to integration and end-to-end tests. This thorough testing provides developers with the assurance that their code will perform correctly in production.

Effective Observability

Once the code is deployed, it's crucial to monitor its performance in real time. Effective observability means having dashboards and monitoring tools that provide instant insights into the system's health. With a quick glance, developers should be able to confirm that everything is functioning as intended. If any issues arise, the developer should be notified immediately, allowing them to address problems before they impact users.

Simple Rollbacks

Even with the best testing and monitoring in place, issues can still occur. In such cases, a team should be able to roll back the deployment effortlessly. The rollback process should be simple and quick, ensuring that any disruptions are minimized and normal service is restored as soon as possible.

Own Your Own Changes

Traditionally, software development followed a sequential process where different teams handled different stages of the software lifecycle. Developers wrote the code, QA teams tested it, and operations teams deployed it. This division often led to delays, miscommunication, and a lack of accountability.

When you are continuously deploying each change in an automated way through to production, the boundaries between each of these roles can blur as you start to move and deliver more quickly. Instead, developers should be accountable for owning their own changes through the software lifecycle to production. They should oversee deployments, ensure adequate QA has occurred, chase reviews, make sure the infrastructure their software is sitting on is sound, and ensure adequate alerting and observability is in place before the change is put in front of users.

This feeling of accountability from developers should improve code quality, but will also improve the speed at which issues are resolved. The developer should have the knowledge and context of their code through the whole lifecycle, rather than a problem pinging around a number of different teams and individuals as they bat an incident around to each other. This extra context should massively reduce bottlenecks in the process as problems get passed around from one team to another, leading to a slicker journey to production, which allows for continuous integration and deployments.

It also fosters better collaboration as a developer interfaces and collaborates with their QA, operations, and Site Reliability Engineering (SRE) teams to ensure they have ticked the boxes they need to.

Be Metrics-Driven

Teams who are driven by, and measure their success with, real-life metrics perform better than teams who do not. When Capital One used DORA metrics to measure and identify their problem areas, they were able to improve their performance by 20 times.[1]

Some of the most important metrics with which you can measure your team's performance are those same DORA metrics:

1. **Deployment frequency** measures how often a team successfully deploys code to production. High-performing teams deploy more frequently, allowing for faster feedback loops and more rapid iterations. This leads to more agile and responsive development practices, enhancing customer satisfaction and market adaptability.

2. **Lead time for changes** tracks the time taken from code commit to deployment. Shorter lead times indicate efficient development processes, allowing teams to respond quickly to changes and new requirements, which is crucial for maintaining a competitive edge.

---

[1] https://waydev.co/dora-metrics

3. **Mean time to recovery (MTTR)** measures how quickly a team can restore service after an incident. Lower MTTR means quicker recovery from failures, minimizing downtime and its associated costs and thus ensuring more reliable service for users.

4. **Change Failure Rate** indicates the percentage of changes that lead to failures in production. A lower rate signifies more robust and stable deployments, which reduces the risk of incidents and improves overall system reliability.

These metrics can help you identify where you need improvement and have provably led to better-performing technology teams, who can better achieve the goals of the organization they're working for.

Goodhart's Law however states that "When a measure becomes a target, it ceases to be a good measure," and that is true here also. Don't just pursue DORA metrics for the sake of hitting metrics, but keep in mind the software goals you're actually trying to achieve as a development team. Measuring performance and being driven by metrics does not mean becoming a slave to metrics and measurements rather than your actual goals and objectives. If you need to deliver a feature by November, and you don't, then shareholders won't care if your mean time to recovery is still great!

Instead, make your goals and objectives measurable. Break your quarterly goals down into measurable OKRs you can track performance against, and keep those in mind alongside your DORA metrics.

Prioritizing Technical Debt

You should also be driven by metrics in terms of bugs and technical debt. Utilize your monitoring and observability platform to ensure you are recording the metrics that matter. If you need to prioritize a bug, you should be able to prioritize it based on the number of users it's actively affecting or the amount of money each particular bug might be costing your business.

AB Testing

AB testing is a helpful way to quickly test ideas that may or may not bring success to the organization. It allows you to serve some users a brand-new feature, styling changes, or UI or copy changes and check that it hits the success metric you've defined for that subset of users before productionizing the change and rolling it out to everyone.

Before starting any AB test, it is crucial to establish clear, achievable, and measurable success metrics for the change you plan to test. Success metrics might include user engagement rates, conversion rates, or time spent on the page. These metrics provide a concrete way to evaluate the effectiveness of the changes and make informed decisions off the back of the test. Ensure that these metrics are straightforward and realistic and can be accurately measured using the tools and analytics available to you.

Once you have these success metrics, it's essential that you have a reliable way to measure the outcomes of your tests against them. You can utilize robust analytics tools to track user interactions and provide precise data on how each version of the feature is performing. Consistent monitoring of both versions will help identify trends and gather sufficient data for analysis, ensuring that the insights gained from the AB test are accurate and actionable. There are AB testing tools like Optimizely that will do some of this for you, but you may want to enhance this with data from analytics tools like Google Analytics.

Once you have established clear success metrics and chosen the appropriate analytics tools to track and measure your user interactions, you can effectively implement AB testing by deploying the variants to different user groups and collecting data on their performance. Compare the performance of each variant against the success metrics and decide whether to fully implement the change, refine it, or discard it based on the metrics you've learned. This data should give you confidence in the decisions your development team is making and allow your product decisions to be metrics-driven.

It is absolutely essential, however, that you have a strong idea of what your success metrics are for a particular change and a reliable and straightforward way to measure your performance against those metrics before you embark on any AB testing. If you do not have these things, then AB testing can just be another bottleneck in your processes slowing down organizational performance.

Autonomy

Successfully implementing continuous integration, and especially continuous deployment, hinges on granting a significant level of autonomy to every member of the development team. This autonomy means that the team operates without external gates, artificial bottlenecks, or change management boards that can slow down the whole process. This requires everyone—developers, managers, and stakeholders—to become very comfortable with the idea that development teams have the autonomy and the freedom to push their code to production any time that they wish.

Embracing Autonomy

Autonomy in a development team means that developers can make decisions and act quickly, without waiting for approvals from external bodies. This speeds up the development process and allows for more rapid iterations and faster delivery of features and fixes. However, with this freedom comes a corresponding level of accountability. Developers must own their changes from development through to production, ensuring that their code is robust and well-tested, meets user requirements, and meets all of the necessary quality and observability standards.

Accountability Without Blame

A critical aspect of this autonomy is accountability. Developers are accountable for the code they push to production, which fosters a sense of ownership and responsibility. However, accountability should not be confused with blame! When issues arise due to changes pushed to production, the focus should be on conducting blameless retrospectives or post-incident reviews. These retrospectives aim to understand what went wrong and how processes can be improved to prevent similar incidents in the future, rather than pointing fingers and assigning blame to individuals.

Blameless retrospectives are essential in creating a safe environment where team members feel comfortable taking risks and making decisions. This approach encourages continuous learning and ongoing improvements to your processes, which are vital components of a successful CI/CD implementation. All focus should be on highlighting these potential process improvements, rather than unnecessarily and ineffectually finding an individual to place blame on.

The Role of Management

Granting autonomy to the development team can be a significant shift for both managers and developers. Managers and stakeholders used to having control over the deployment process may initially resist this change. They may worry about the risks associated with allowing developers to push code to production without additional oversight. Similarly, developers accustomed to relying on change managers or QA teams for approvals may feel uncomfortable with their new responsibilities.

To address these concerns, it's essential to

- **Communicate Clearly:** Explain the benefits of autonomy to all stakeholders. Highlight how it leads to faster delivery, more efficient processes, and higher-quality software.

- **Provide Training:** Offer training and support to help developers adapt to their new roles. This can include workshops on best practices for CI/CD, code reviews, and automated testing.

- **Showcase Successes:** Share success stories from teams that have successfully adopted autonomy. Demonstrating tangible improvements in productivity and software quality can help build confidence in the new approach.

- **Foster a Supportive Environment:** Encourage a culture of collaboration and mutual support. Ensure that developers know they can seek help and guidance from their peers and managers as they adjust to their new responsibilities.

Managers play a crucial role in facilitating this transition. They need to set the tone by promoting a culture of trust and empowerment and allow every member of the team to have the safety and comfort they need to act in an autonomous way. This might involve

- **Encouraging Experimentation:** Allow developers to experiment with new tools, techniques, and processes. Celebrate successes and treat failures as learning opportunities.

- **Providing Resources:** Ensure that developers have access to the resources they need to succeed, such as training, tools, and time for learning and experimentation.

- **Removing Obstacles:** Actively work to remove any remaining bottlenecks or barriers that might hinder the team's autonomy. This can involve streamlining processes, reducing unnecessary bureaucracy, and advocating for the team's needs with higher management.

Building Developer Confidence

It is expected that some managers and stakeholders might not like this newfound autonomy the development team now wields. But you should also be prepared for developers not being used to working in this way either. Developers who have worked in projects where they have regularly thrown changes over the wall to a change manager or a QA team may indeed be slightly uncomfortable with the new status quo and might require some persuasion and management to help to embody the behaviors a developer working on fast-paced project needs.

For developers to thrive in an autonomous environment, they need to feel confident in their abilities and supported by their team. Here are some strategies to build this confidence:

- **Mentorship and Peer Learning:** Establish mentorship programs where experienced developers can guide and support their less experienced colleagues. Encourage peer learning and knowledge sharing through regular team meetings, code reviews, and collaborative problem-solving sessions.

- **Incremental Changes:** Start with small, incremental changes to build confidence gradually. As developers become more comfortable with their new responsibilities, they can take on more significant and complex tasks.

- **Regular Feedback:** Provide regular, constructive
  feedback to help developers improve their skills
  and processes. Celebrate achievements and provide
  guidance on areas for improvement.

By granting development teams the freedom to push their code to production without external bottlenecks, organizations can achieve faster delivery, higher-quality software, and more efficient processes. This autonomy must be coupled with a strong sense of accountability, along with blameless retrospectives, to foster continuous learning and improvement. While the transition to an autonomous environment may be challenging, clear communication, training, and a supportive culture can help overcome resistance and build confidence.

Psychological Safety

In 2012, Google began a project they named Project Aristotle. The idea behind Project Aristotle was to examine hundreds of internal teams at Google and half a century of academic research to attempt to determine the specific patterns and behaviors that correlated, and perhaps even drove, certain teams to perform better than others. Their hypothesis was that successful teams would be made up of the best performers and experienced leaders and have unfettered access to unlimited resources. Their findings were actually quite different.

The team used lots of different measures and attributes to try and determine what made up a good team. They looked at all kinds of attributes—whether it was beneficial for members of the team to be friends outside of work, whether they had the same hobbies, similar backgrounds, similar personality types. They found no evidence that the makeup of members on a team made any difference. "We had lots of data, but there was nothing showing that a mix of specific personality types or skills or backgrounds made any difference. The 'who' part of the equation didn't seem to matter," said Abeer Dubey, one of the leaders of the project, before later saying, "At Google, we're good at finding patterns. There weren't strong patterns here."[2]

But if who is on a team wasn't a statistically significant signifier of the success of a team at Google, what is? The researchers went on to look at what behaviors and cultural indicators made a difference to the performance of a team and discovered some interesting patterns. They discovered that how a team worked together was much a more important factor than the individuals they placed on those teams (or as Aristotle himself said: "The whole is greater than the sum of its parts").

The most important cultural factors of a high-performing team were, in order of importance:

1. **Psychological safety**

   Psychological safety was found to be the most statistically significant signifier of whether a team would perform well at Google. This refers to how dire members of a team perceive the potential (real or imagined) consequences of risky behavior could be to their reputation or relationships within their team. A team with a high level of psychological safety will have team members who ask questions, admit mistakes, raise ideas, or speak up in meetings, without any fear of ridicule or punishment or negative reputational impact.

2. **Mutual trust**

   Team members on Google's best team displayed a good level of trust in each other.

---

[2] https://www.nytimes.com/2016/02/28/magazine/what-google-learned-from-its-quest-to-build-the-perfect-team.html

3. **Structure and clarity**

    Teams understand their requirements, team processes, and desired outcomes.

4. **Meaning of work**

    Team members feel a sense of purpose in the work their team is undertaking.

5. **Impact**

    An important signifier of high performance was that the members of the team knew that their work was making a significant impact and how the team's outcomes fit into the larger mission at the organization.

What Google had actually discovered was that it was far more important that members of a team were coming to work feeling comfortable that they could be themselves and with a real sense of purpose in their work. Those things were a much more significant identifier of whether their team would reach their goals than the seniority or location or type of work or educational background of the members of that team.

The findings of this report are hugely informative as to what it takes to succeed in implementing continuous integration and continuous deployment. CI/CD practices require communication, trust, and autonomy, and team members absolutely need to feel psychological safety to successfully display any of those behaviors at work in any real capacity.

Winning People Over

It's important to bring managers, stakeholders, QA, and indeed the development team along for the ride when implementing CI/CD. CI/CD relies heavily on good collaboration and communication throughout the team, and if you don't have this, you won't achieve success.

In 2007, Jeffrey Hiatt and Timothy Creasey looked at the top reasons employees and managers might resist change. Some of the reasons were a fear of the unknown, a fear of losing control and authority, lack of job security, comfort in the status quo, and having had no involvement in the solution design. All of these reasons might cause resistance to your attempts at implementing CI/CD at your organization.

It's important to consider these potential drivers to resistance when communicating and implementing your ideas.

Engage and Involve

It can be tricky to engage colleagues who are skeptical of change. This may be because they don't believe in the benefits of CI/CD (these people should be easy to persuade[3]) or, more likely, because they are resistant to change and are used to the status quo. Persuading these more conservative colleagues can be a lot more frustrating, as a lot of their challenge is coming from a more emotional place.

It's important not to get frustrated though! These people work for your organization because their input matters, and it can be counterintuitive to react stubbornly from your own emotional place. In actual fact, everyone is striving for the same thing—success for your team and organization—so try to engage and involve your colleagues.

The easiest way to win your conservative skeptics over is to collaborate with them! You should sit down and really listen to your colleagues' gripes with the new approach.

Perhaps your colleague is a QA, who believes CD is far too risky for your organization and believes that the manual regression testing they carry out before each release is absolutely fundamental to the success of your organization. It's best to hear them out. Perhaps they are partly right!

---

[3] See Chapter 1 for "The Science Behind CI/CD"

It's a good idea in this situation to sit down with your skeptical QA colleague and talk to them about exactly what they do in terms of manual regression testing and what steps they think the new process would be missing. Why not automate, or ask your skeptical colleague to help automate, these exact steps? Pull this person in as the colleague accountable for making sure these automated tests reach the desired quality gate. After all, QAs are ultimately the experts on software quality at your organization. Use them!

A good byproduct of this (as found by Creasey and Hiatt in 2007) is that if you do bring people along for the ride and allow them to help actually design the solution, they are then less likely to be resistant to the proposed changes. Your colleagues might also have really valuable input that you wouldn't otherwise have heard.

Make sure you know your audience before you engage and try to influence your colleagues! Some people's resistance is caused by a concern about job security, some by a fear of the unknown, and some by genuine concerns in your proposed solutions. Ascertaining the driver behind any resistance you get implementing CI/CD can help you address this resistance properly.

Highlight the Benefits

If the reason behind resistance is a genuine concern with the proposed solution of CI/CD, then clear and effective communication should be able to overcome this. If you can present the benefits of CI/CD in a clear and concise way, citing scientific evidence, anecdotes, and visual aids to convey your ideas, you should be halfway there.

There are common arguments against CI/CD that you should be able to easily prepare for. Arguments like "It's more risky" or "Won't we just spend all day making sure the build is working?" or "We don't have time to tackle that right now with all the features we're building"—these can be fairly simply rebutted with evidence and facts, and you can prepare those answers beforehand.

But there might also be specific reasons that CI/CD might be difficult on your technical stack or with your organization. By way of an example, I have worked at organizations that require extra levels of approval for regulatory reasons, and this was used as an argument by some of my colleagues as to why CI/CD wouldn't be a good fit for the project. After every change was merged, it was deployed to an environment where a change management process would begin and sign-offs would be collected. What we did instead was streamline this change management process as much as possible (as discussed earlier, the DORA research program found that in fact change management processes can be shown to be inefficient, can slow down delivery, and can even increase risk), and then we moved the remaining approval processes so that they happened before merge alongside the code review process. This change meant that the main branch was clear for fully tested, releasable code, allowing the project to start gaining the CI/CD benefits of faster time to market, more reliable software, a higher likelihood of hitting organizational goals, etc.

Another great way to illustrate the benefits of your approach is to trial it on a lower-risk part of the system. This can be easier to get buy-in and allow you to really show the benefits and ease of transition in a real-world setting.

Get Alignment

It's important to get broad alignment from the team for your ideas. CI/CD doesn't work unless people really buy into the cultural and technical changes that are needed. Collaboration and good communication are vital to a successful development team, and aligning a team to a new way of working will be a good test of your ability to collaborate and communicate effectively.

Make sure you truly listen to concerns and don't just pay lip service to doing so. Mike Cohn, in his book *Succeeding with Agile*, suggests appointing a chief skeptic—someone well liked and with influence among those resistant to change—to distil down all of the dissenting arguments and opinions and allow you to counter them and then help you communicate them back out among peers.

You should also make sure you're highlighting how this change in ways of working aligns with organizational goals. CI/CD is not something that is just done for technical, nerdy reasons, but is scientifically proven to improve your development team's likelihood of helping your organization reach their wider goals, so make sure to both highlight that and measure your success against it.

Key Takeaways

- **Cultural Change Is Critical:** Successful adoption of CI/CD practices is not just technical but requires significant cultural shifts. Teams must foster collaboration, cross-functional integration, and continuous improvement.

- **Pipeline Stability Is Essential:** The build pipeline is the backbone of CI/CD, and its stability must be prioritized. Immediate action should be taken when issues arise, with collaborative efforts to resolve problems quickly to maintain productivity and workflow efficiency.

- **Small, Frequent Releases:** Agile methodologies and delivering small, incremental changes are key to CI/CD. This approach enables quicker feedback, faster iterations, and reduced risk during integration and deployment.

- **Blameless Culture:** When things go wrong, it's important to focus on process improvements rather than assigning individual blame. Postmortems and retrospectives should be conducted in a constructive way that encourages learning and continuous process enhancement.

- **Limit Work in Progress (WIP):** High-performing teams prioritize completing tasks over starting new ones, reducing bottlenecks and improving collaboration. This requires shifting from individual accomplishments to team-focused success.

- **Emphasize Communication:** Effective communication through practices like pair programming, mob programming, and synchronous pull requests enhances collaboration and helps teams navigate through the complexities of continuous deployment.

- **Autonomy and Accountability:** Teams should be empowered with the autonomy to push their code to production but must also be accountable for the quality, testing, and performance of their changes.

- **Metrics-Driven Improvement:** Teams should use metrics like deployment frequency, lead time for changes, and mean time to recovery (MTTR) to measure success and drive continuous improvement. However, metrics should always serve the larger organizational goals.

- **Psychological Safety:** Creating an environment of psychological safety where team members can voice concerns and admit mistakes without fear of blame is essential for a high-performing team.

- **Winning People Over:** Resistance to change is common when implementing CI/CD, so it's vital to engage, involve, and align stakeholders, ensuring that the benefits are clearly communicated and understood across the organization.

By embracing these cultural shifts and technical practices, teams can leverage CI/CD to deliver software faster and more efficiently. In the next chapter, we'll discuss how to also leverage these practices safely, making sure that speed and efficiency doesn't come at the expense of safety and stability.

CHAPTER 4

Implementing CI/CD Safely

By automating the integration, testing, and deployment processes, CI/CD pipelines can streamline workflows, reduce manual errors, and ensure that code changes are quickly and reliably moved from development to production. However, with great power comes great responsibility. The speed and automation provided by CI/CD can also introduce significant risks if not implemented with a strong focus on safety and reliability.

The drive for pace and efficiency should never come at the expense of software reliability and comprehensive testing. This chapter focuses on the essential practices and strategies for implementing CI/CD pipelines without compromising on those things. We will explore the methodologies that help maintain high standards of quality—methodologies such as rigorous automated testing, continuous monitoring, and systematic rollback procedures.

While the benefits of a move toward CI/CD practices are clear, it is vital that you achieve a balance between speed and reliability, with the ultimate goal being the delivery of high-quality, safe, and reliable software, delivered at pace.

© Tommy Clark 2025
T. Clark, *CI/CD Unleashed*, Apress Pocket Guides,
https://doi.org/10.1007/979-8-8688-1209-5_4

Test, Test, Test

If CI/CD is to work, it is absolutely fundamental that testing is built into every stage of the software development lifecycle. Testing in CI/CD is not just an afterthought or a separate phase that follows development. Instead, it is an integral part of every step in the lifecycle. From the initial stages of development to the final deployment, testing ensures that each change, no matter how small, is thoroughly vetted before it reaches the end user.

You should have an automated test suite that adheres to the testing pyramid, with a strong foundation of unit tests that should have been written alongside the delivery of each unit of code via a process of test-driven development. You will then have integration tests covering integration of these units and functional or end-to-end tests at the top of the pyramid providing light-touch coverage of entire user flows. It is expected that developers will run these automated tests on their local development environment many times a day, so they must be written with that requirement in mind.

Automated performance tests can also be included in the pipeline to ensure that new changes still perform as expected under load, particularly if you have client SLAs (service-level agreements) that you're obliged to comply with.

All tests in your pipeline must be reliable, efficient, and a good indicator that your change will work in production. If they aren't doing those things, then they aren't of value and should be removed, fixed, or changed.

If you have QA engineers in your team, they shouldn't be blockers in the process or gatekeepers of quality. Quality and testing needs to be built in throughout the process, and that means every member of the team taking ownership and accountability for quality. Your QA colleague should be working in a consultative capacity, making sure that you are tackling quality in the correct way strategically as a team, and providing advice on the best way to assure quality on specific features and parts of the system.

Your QA should not be manually testing your service as a blocker to a change being put live. This is an inefficient and unreliable anti-pattern. There is a place for manual testing, but that is where you are using it as an exploratory tool in order to check for user interface and usability issues and looking out for missed or misunderstood requirements.

An Example Pipeline

Every use case is different, as every project has a completely different set of unique needs and requirements for its pipeline. For instance, a pipeline for a financial trading system, which requires rigorous security measures and low-latency performance, might be vastly different from a pipeline for a small e-commerce website, which might prioritize user experience and rapid feature deployment.

But there are a set of common steps one would expect to find in the majority of CD pipelines for most applications, ensuring that despite the unique needs of different projects and organizations, the fundamental principles of continuous integration and deployment are upheld, enabling a software team to practice continuous delivery safely and reliably.

Figure 4-1 illustrates a typical example software pipeline for a project using continuous deployment, highlighting these critical stages within a pipeline.

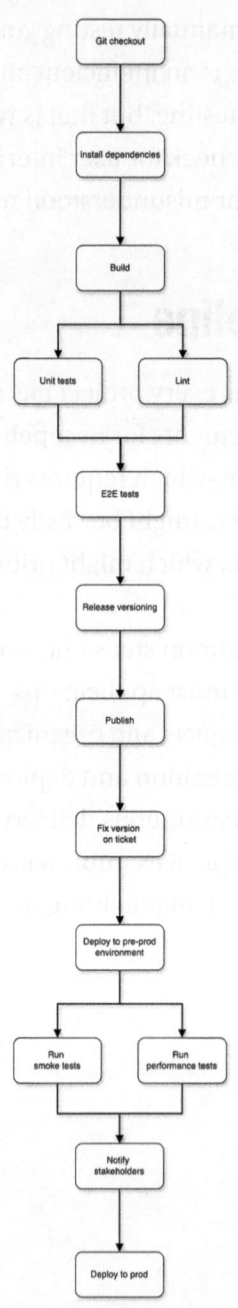

Figure 4-1. *An example of a CI/CD pipeline*

SCM Checkout

The first step of your CI/CD pipeline will be to check your source code out from SCM (most likely Git). You can pull straight from main or, for a branch build, pull the git ref that relates to the HEAD of your branch.

Install Dependencies

The next step is to download and install the dependencies and external libraries that your application needs to be able to run. This might be a command like "yarn install" or a "pip install -r requirements.txt" depending on the technology in your stack. You might want to pull these libraries through a package management system like JFrog Artifactory or Sonatype Nexus to provide more reliability, control, and consistency around your development teams' dependency downloads.

Build

The next step, now that you have the source code and all dependencies installed, will be to build your code. You'll want to minimize the time this build takes by using build caches (GitHub Actions or nx caches or Gradle cache), docker base images that you may have saved as artifacts from previous builds, or docker layers so you are just rebuilding the application layer of your docker image. Make sure this build is reliable and idempotent. If two different people run this build with the same inputs at different times, the output of the build must be identical.

In the book *Site Reliability Engineering*, written by members of Google's SRE team, they mention hermetic builds. They take consistency and repeatability one step further by making sure that builds are insensitive to libraries and software installed on the machine building the software. They note that "instead, builds depend on known versions of build tools, such as compilers, and dependencies, such as libraries. The build process is self-contained and must not rely on services that are external to the build environment."

Unit Tests

This is where you run your unit tests. You will want to run all of these every time there is a change anywhere in your application code. These should be fast, reliable, and idempotent. If there are tests in here that occasionally flake or fail, spend time fixing them, or remove them altogether. You don't need 100% test coverage (quality over quantity), but make sure your team is utilizing TDD for good (and high-quality) test coverage and fail the build at this point if you have dropped below an agreed test coverage percentage threshold.

Lint

You can lint your code in parallel with the above test suite. This will allow everyone on the team to easily read, understand, maintain, and change the codebase. A consistent code style can save time and reduce the risk of introducing bugs or errors during code changes.

End-to-End Tests

Run your end-to-end and integration tests. These are higher up the testing pyramid than your unit tests, and so you shouldn't expect high coverage from this test suite, but ensure they cover the main journeys through your application code. Your QA should be able to help you ascertain and map out what these key journeys are and help ensure automated coverage of them.

Version

Now that your code has been built and tested, it's ready to be versioned. You might decide to do this in a number of ways, but semantic versioning is an industry standard that clearly communicates the nature of the release and makes clear any breaking changes, by using a MAJOR.MINOR. PATCH convention (e.g., 1.7.3). You can use "conventional commits" in conjunction with tooling and libraries to automate the versioning process depending on the commits in the release.

Once you have a version, you will want to git tag your code. This allows you to pull the repository containing the code, infrastructure, and config exactly as it was for your release. This is important for auditing, investigating incidents, and fixing bugs.

You will also want to tag or name your artifacts, so that you can pull the built software you need for release.

Publish Artifacts

Publishing these newly tagged build artifacts allows you to make the output of the build process available for subsequent stages of your pipeline (or external systems if you are building or deploying libraries or software that doesn't need deploying to a server). You might publish your artifact to a package manager like Artifactory/Nexus, or this step may be you publishing docker images to cloud storage or a docker registry like AWS ECR. This step allows you to store and archive build artifacts, publish them for use elsewhere, and/or use them in the upcoming deploy steps of your pipeline.

Add Fix Versions to Tickets

Adding a fix version to a Jira ticket in a CI/CD pipeline involves associating a specific software version with a bug or feature request. This practice helps track which code changes resolve particular issues and enables stakeholders to easily identify the impact of a release.

Fix versions allow developers to trace the progress of bug fixes and enhancements throughout the development and deployment process and might help you to generate changelogs containing every ticket that has made it into the release. By linking tickets to specific versions, teams can quickly determine which issues are addressed in each release, making it easier to communicate with customers and stakeholders about bug fixes and new features.

Deploy to Test or Pre-production Environments

You'll now be ready to deploy your software to an environment. This step will involve making the built software and infrastructure available for use in a non-live environment, such as a test or pre-production environment. The deployment process typically includes provisioning the necessary infrastructure and configuration and deploying the built and versioned artifact.

How you provision your infrastructure as part of this stage will depend on your deployment strategy, and different deployment strategies can be used to achieve different goals, such as

- **Blue/green deployment:** This will involve deploying the new version of the application to a separate environment (the "green" environment), while the existing version continues to run in the production environment (the "blue" environment). Once the new version has been tested and verified, traffic is switched from the blue environment to the green environment.

- **Rolling deployment:** This strategy involves deploying the new version of the application to a subset of servers or instances in your environment. Once the new version has been tested and verified on this subset, it is deployed to the remaining servers or instances.

- **Canary deployment:** This strategy involves deploying the new version of the application to a small percentage of users. Once the new version has been tested and verified by these users, it is deployed to the remaining users.

  You may want to test this deployment process on a pre-production environment, but there is no real benefit of canary deploying to a staging environment, so make sure you configure low thresholds for continuing the deployment so that you don't slow down the build for little benefit.

The choice of deployment strategy will depend on the specific needs and requirements of the application and the organization, but by the end of this step, your code should be in an environment and ready to serve traffic to internal users and testers.

It's worth noting that while this is a good time to test your production deployment process, you get little benefit from a rolling or canary deployment in a test environment, so make sure you are configuring your deployment in staging with numbers that provide a good balance between giving you confidence for your production release and speed of your build and release process.

Run Smoke Tests

Smoke testing in a CI/CD pipeline involves running a series of automated tests to quickly verify the basic functionality and stability of a software application or system after a new build or deployment. These tests are typically designed to ensure that critical features are working as expected and that the system is responsive and healthy. This is the very top of the testing pyramid and so should be a very light-touch test that just checks key journeys or features to make sure the system is behaving as expected now in an environment.

Smoke tests often include checking health endpoints or liveness and readiness probes, which are mechanisms used to assess the availability and responsiveness of an application or service. Health endpoints are typically simple HTTP requests that return a status code indicating the health of the system, while liveness and readiness probes might be more sophisticated mechanisms that can be used to determine if an application is ready to accept traffic.

Smoke testing in a CI/CD pipeline is important because it provides a quick and efficient way to catch major issues early in the deployment process, before they can impact users or customers, and introduces a way to determine that your deployment has successfully completed. By automating these tests as part of the pipeline, teams can ensure that any problems with a new build or deployment are identified and addressed promptly, reducing the risk of production outages or service disruptions.

Run Performance Tests

Performance testing in a CI/CD pipeline involves evaluating the performance characteristics of an application or system under load to ensure it meets the required performance criteria. It helps identify bottlenecks, performance regressions, and scalability issues early in the development process.

By integrating performance testing into the CI/CD pipeline, teams can automate the testing process, ensuring that performance is consistently validated with each code change or configuration update. This proactive approach helps prevent performance issues from reaching production, resulting in a more stable and reliable application or system.

Notify Stakeholders and Add Fix Versions

If this is a production pipeline (rather than a branch build), then notifying stakeholders in a CI/CD pipeline can be useful for keeping them informed about the status and progress of your deployments. It's a nonessential but potentially helpful step in your pipeline.

There are several ways you might want to notify stakeholders. You might send an automated notification to teams or individuals via platforms like Microsoft Teams, Slack, or email or automatically creating and sharing a changelog. However you choose to do this should not add manual steps or toil for your development team and should be done in an automated, consistent, and repeatable way.

Automatically notifying your stakeholders in real time about successful and failed deployments can help promote transparency, allowing stakeholders to stay informed about the deployment process and any potential issues. It can help facilitate collaboration and enable stakeholders to provide feedback or raise concerns promptly. Don't feel compelled to notify people if you think it will just add noise or be ignored or annoying.

At this stage, you will also want to add the deploy version to the Jira ticket. This is essential as it provides a clear record of the deployed version associated with a particular issue or feature. This information can be valuable for tracking changes, identifying potential issues, and ensuring that everyone is on the same page.

Deploy to Your Production Environment

The final stage! Deploy to real users! Similarly to the above step, this step will only be run for a production pipeline (and not if this particular pipeline run is just to ensure a build is okay to merge).

This stage should be almost an exact repeat of your pre-production deployment, perhaps with some different configurations, such as slightly different numbers configured for any canary deployment stages you might have.

This should only ever be done from your main branch (or trunk) and never from fix, release, or feature branches.

Maintaining Reliability in Production

Automating the deployment of every change to production, or deploying often, may require teams to behave differently in order to maintain reliability of their services in production. Some organizations don't require developers to be responsible or accountable for operating their software in production. Some developers may not even be involved in the process of maintaining and operating production. In these old-fashioned models, where a development team might throw their software over the wall to an Ops team, continuous integration, and certainly continuous deployment, likely won't work very well.

In organizations like this, where a development team solely has an interest in developing new features for users and an operations team solely has an interest in operating production in a stable and reliable way, there will naturally be conflict. Key members of Google's site reliability team wrote in their book *Site Reliability Engineering* about their findings that 70% of production incidents come from changes to production. If you have a development team that desires these production changes without a care for reliability and an operations team that desires stability in production without any care for delivering new features for customers, then you will continue to experience this conflict.

What we want with continuous deployment, however, is what *Site Reliability Engineering* describes as "maximum change velocity without violating a service's SLO."

SLIs, SLOs, and SLAs

To know whether or not you're violating the SLO of your service, you need a measurable SLO. Our understanding of what our end users need and want helps inform our SLIs (service-level indicators), SLOs (service-level objectives), and SLAs (service-level agreements).

Service-Level Indicator (SLI)

An SLI is a specific, measurable value that indicates the performance of a service. It is a quantitative measure that reflects the health or performance of a particular aspect of the service. SLIs are typically defined in terms of metrics like latency, availability, throughput, error rate, or response time. For example, the SLI for availability might be calculated as the percentage of successful requests out of the total requests made.

Examples:

- **SLI for Availability:** If 999 out of 1,000 requests are successful, the availability SLI would be 99.9%.

- **SLI for Latency:** If the average response time for a service is 200 milliseconds, that is your latency SLI.

Service-Level Objective (SLO)

An SLO is a target value or range for an SLI. It defines what level of performance or reliability is considered acceptable by the service provider. SLOs are used to set expectations for the service and guide operational priorities. An SLO is usually set based on business requirements and customer expectations, and it serves as a benchmark to ensure that the service is performing as expected.

Example:

- **SLO for Availability:** An SLO might state that the service should have 99.9% availability over a monthly period.

- **SLO for Latency:** An SLO might require that 95% of requests should have a latency of under 300 milliseconds.

Service-Level Agreement (SLA)

An SLA is a formal agreement between a service provider and a customer that defines the expected level of service. It includes one or more SLOs and often specifies the consequences or penalties if the agreed-upon service levels are not met. SLAs are typically contractual and can include various aspects like uptime guarantees, response times, or support availability. The SLA outlines what happens if the SLOs are not achieved, often including financial penalties or credits.

Example:

- **SLA for Availability:** An SLA might guarantee 99.9% uptime, and if the service falls below this threshold, the customer might be entitled to a refund or service credit.

- **SLA for Support:** An SLA might promise a response from customer support within two hours for critical issues, with penalties if this time frame is not met.

Service-level indicators (SLIs) provide us with specific metrics or indicators that provide measurable data on the performance of a service, so we can measure whether or not we're achieving success in terms of our production performance. Service-level objectives (SLOs) set the target or threshold for these SLIs, determining what level of service performance is considered acceptable, while service-level agreements (SLAs) formalize these SLOs into a contractual agreement between the service provider and the customer, often including penalties or other consequences if the agreed-upon service levels are not met. If you have an SLA without any consequences if you don't meet it, you're more likely looking at an SLO instead. All three of these types of measures help us measure and quantify our reliability in production.

Without measuring reliability, it's difficult to improve reliability in any metrics-driven, quantifiable way.

Implementing an Error Budget

Now that we can measure our performance in production, we can consider our room for error. As mentioned earlier, when a development team is pushing for features and an operations team is pushing for reliability, there can naturally be conflict. Google, as described in the book *Site Reliability Engineering*, resolved this conflict by implementing an error budget.

The idea is that 100% is *pretty much always* the wrong reliability target for software systems. For almost all software, there is no perceptible difference to a user between 99.999% and 100% availability. There'll likely be services and systems in between your user and your software (phone lines, laptops, servers, Internet connections, power grids) that are collectively less than 99.999% available, and so there is often little point in striving for 100% at extra cost to the business but no tangible benefit to the user.

Instead, setting an availability target at, say, 99.9% gives you a 0.1% error budget to spend as you please. Most likely you will spend that error budget on driving changes for users to achieve extra value for the business. Google uses this error budget to drive innovation by allowing an operations/SRE team and a development team to align more in terms of their goals. As they put it, "SRE's goal is no longer 'zero outages'; rather, SREs and product developers aim to spend the error budget getting maximum feature velocity" (*Site Reliability Engineering*, 2016).

Aiming for 100% availability doesn't just stifle innovation though. It is also a waste of resource. Perhaps you need to provision extra capacity (in terms of actual servers or cloud compute) at all times to ensure 100% availability, which 99.99% of the time is completely redundant. You might need to also invest time and effort from reliability engineering teams, working on redundancy and process to guarantee that extra 0.01%. There's an opportunity cost to having engineers work on these problems rather than driving innovation for the business and its users.

Sometimes there's a calculation to be made. Does the additional revenue or positive user impact of that extra 0.01% or 0.001% offset the cost of reaching that number? The answer to this question will help you decide your SLIs, SLOs, and SLAs and, therefore, your budget for error.

DevOps and SRE

Businesses are increasingly relying on their software infrastructure to deliver value. As software systems grow more complex and their role more integral to organizational success, we have needed better ways to maintain that infrastructure. Enter DevOps and Site Reliability Engineering (SRE)—two complementary methodologies designed to bridge the gap between development and operations while ensuring that high-velocity delivery does not come at the cost of stability and safety.

Both DevOps and SRE are often considered two sides of the same coin, with shared objectives but distinct approaches. At their core, these practices seek to enable fast, reliable software delivery and mitigate the risks associated with rapid change. They also both help break down that natural conflict between Dev and Ops.

Let's explore how DevOps and SRE can coexist and complement one another, fostering an engineering culture that values both speed and stability.

Velocity and Safety in Production

One of the core tenets of both DevOps and SRE is that high velocity and safety in production are not mutually exclusive. Traditionally, speed was seen as a risk—rushing features into production without sufficient testing or proper deployment processes could lead to outages, bugs, or security vulnerabilities. The DevOps movement aimed to dispel this myth by introducing automation and embedding operations and the maintenance of production into the development team itself and enabling safe and reliable continuous deployment.

Meanwhile, SRE (pioneered by Google and discussed in the book *Site Reliability Engineering*) takes a similar approach but introduces an additional focus on reliability. The key to achieving both speed and safety is becoming comfortable with the production environment. This comfort is rooted in automation, visibility, and a cultural shift that prioritizes learning from failures rather than fearing them.

As we've discussed, research from the DevOps Research and Assessment (DORA) group provides evidence that teams who are comfortable operating in production environments achieve higher performance. They reduce downtime, increase the pace of feature delivery, and maintain high levels of reliability. DevOps teams often rely on monitoring, logging, and alerting systems to gain real-time insights into the state of their systems. This means they can quickly identify issues and remediate them, turning production into a safer space for experimentation and innovation rather than a fragile place to fear.

In SRE, this comfort in production is often helped further by introducing the error budgets we spoke about. By defining the acceptable level of failure up front, SRE teams can balance the competing needs of velocity and reliability. If the error budget is depleted, development teams focus on stability and reliability until the system is back within acceptable limits. If not, more innovation and features can be pushed without additional risk.

The ability to deploy confidently and remediate issues swiftly allows teams to move fast without breaking things. Having the confidence to make changes in production is absolutely key to that.

Time Allocation: 50% on Operations

One of the principles outlined in Google's SRE model is the notion that site reliability engineers should spend no more than 50% of their time on operational tasks or toil. The other 50% must be spent on engineering project work that will either reduce future toil or add service features. This might be specifically focusing on improving the system's reliability through automation, tooling, process improvement, or perhaps even actual feature work.

The repetitive, manual nature of operations can lead to burnout, stagnation, and inefficiency, while—instead—the SRE philosophy encourages a shift from reactive firefighting to proactive engineering solutions that eliminate problems at their source. Operational tasks—such as monitoring alerts, resolving incidents, and managing on-call rotations— are of course necessary, but they shouldn't dominate an SRE's time.

This balance between operational and engineering work is essential for reducing toil—those repetitive tasks that do not add lasting value. Toil includes tasks like manually restarting services, manually responding to predictable alerts, performing routine deployments without automation, and other soul-destroying and boring tasks that an operations engineer might have to carry out. Reducing toil not only frees up time but also fosters innovation and prevents burnout.

SREs and DevOps engineers should spend more time building systems that solve problems for good, rather than constantly applying temporary fixes.

Engineering-First Mindset

Both DevOps and SRE share an engineering-first mindset, which is central to their success. An engineering-first approach means that teams approach operational challenges with a mindset rooted in software engineering practices. This includes rigorous automation, testing, and continuous improvement.

In the DevOps paradigm, this engineering-first mentality is demonstrated by automating infrastructure, integrating testing and security directly into the CI/CD pipeline, and treating infrastructure as code. Code isn't limited to the application itself but extends to how environments are provisioned, configured, and managed. Teams write code to define their infrastructure, monitor it, and ensure it behaves as expected.

SRE takes this engineering-first approach and applies it to reliability and operations. The core belief is that every operational problem can eventually be engineered away. For example, if an SRE finds themselves repeatedly dealing with the same alert, instead of treating the symptom each time, they are encouraged to build a system that automatically resolves the issue or prevents it from happening in the first place.

This engineering-first mindset is what separates DevOps and SRE from traditional IT operations. Instead of focusing solely on responding to incidents, SREs and DevOps engineers think in terms of building reliable systems from the ground up. It's about problem-solving through code and automation, not just reacting to problems as they arise.

Reducing Toil and Increasing Automation

One of the key outcomes of an engineering-first mindset is a strong emphasis on reducing toil. As mentioned earlier, toil refers to the manual, repetitive tasks that are required to keep systems running but do not contribute to long-term value. Reducing toil is a fundamental goal for both DevOps and SRE because it allows teams to focus on higher-value engineering work that improves the overall system.

In SRE, reducing toil is not just a goal—it's a mandate. Google's SRE guidelines suggest that toil should not exceed 50% of an SRE's time. This means that SREs actively seek out opportunities to automate, streamline, and simplify operational processes. For example, rather than manually scaling servers during traffic spikes, SREs would implement auto-scaling mechanisms that adjust resources automatically based on demand.

In the DevOps world, reducing toil is often achieved through automation and infrastructure as code. Tools like Ansible, Terraform, and Kubernetes allow DevOps teams to automate the provisioning and management of infrastructure, ensuring that environments are consistent, repeatable, and easily scalable. The automation of deployment pipelines, monitoring setups, and incident response processes further reduces the burden of manual work.

As systems grow more complex, the need for automation becomes even more critical. A fully automated pipeline ensures that code can be tested, validated, and deployed consistently across environments without human intervention. Monitoring systems automatically detect anomalies and trigger automated responses, such as scaling up services or rolling back deployments.

Reducing toil also plays a key role in improving team morale and effectiveness. By minimizing repetitive, manual work, teams can focus on creative problem-solving and innovation—work that not only benefits the business but also keeps engineers engaged and motivated.

The Difference Between DevOps and SRE

While DevOps and SRE share many similarities, they differ in their focus and approach. DevOps is more of a cultural and collaborative movement aimed at breaking down silos between development and operations teams, emphasizing automation, continuous integration, and deployment. It is a broad methodology that encourages all teams within the software delivery lifecycle to work together more effectively.

SRE, on the other hand, is a specific implementation of DevOps principles with a heavy focus on reliability. SRE originated at Google as a way to apply software engineering practices to operations work. The goal is to ensure that systems are reliable and scalable while maintaining a high pace of innovation. SRE formalizes this through the concepts we've spoken about—error budgets, service-level objectives (SLOs), and a strict emphasis on reducing toil.

In simple terms, DevOps is about breaking down barriers between development and operations to enable faster and more reliable software delivery. SRE takes this further by applying engineering rigor to operations, ensuring that reliability is not sacrificed in the pursuit of speed. The Google SRE book describes SRE itself as a specific implementation of DevOps with some extensions.

Both represent a significant shift in how software systems are built, maintained, and operated. By prioritizing engineering, automation, and a cultural shift toward collaboration, these methodologies ensure that teams can deliver software at high velocity without compromising reliability or safety. The key to success lies in becoming comfortable in production— knowing that with the right automation, monitoring, and error budgets, it's possible to achieve both speed and stability.

As technology continues to evolve, the lines between development and operations should continue to blur, and the practices of DevOps and SRE will become increasingly intertwined. Together, they form the foundation of modern software delivery, enabling organizations to innovate, deliver, and deploy software quickly while keeping their systems robust, reliable, and resilient.

Monitoring

Monitoring is a hugely important way to maintain reliability and safety while deploying continuously to production. It is essential for ensuring that the rapid pace of changes does not compromise the quality and reliability of your software or the experience of your end users.

Monitoring refers to the observation and tracking of your software system's performance and behavior. It involves collecting and analyzing the data related to your software and the infrastructure your software is hosted on. This could be collecting metrics on CPU and memory usage, response times, and error rates, or it could be collecting custom metrics on certain user interactions. You can then use monitoring tools to build dashboards around these metrics, alert on anomalies, and help diagnose issues. This allows you to either proactively identify potential problems by checking logs, dashboards, and metrics or react to alerts that inform you automatically if users are being impacted by the poor performance of your service.

When your service does go down or becomes unavailable, you should be the first to know. The development team should be informed automatically, so that the problem can be rectified. Developers who are on call should be informed of a triggered alert and should have the knowledge, access, authority, and confidence in production to do what's needed to bring the system back online.

Alerting

Your automated alerts should be set up to alert only when a human needs to actually do something, right now, in order to either fix something that has already gone wrong or something that is about to go wrong. As Google's *Site Reliability Engineering* tells us, "Monitoring should never require a human to interpret any part of the alerting domain. Instead, software should do the interpreting, and humans should be notified only when they need to take action."

When humans have needed to take immediate action in response to a triggered alert, postmortems should be held to determine why human interaction was needed in order to keep the service online. You should review the incident, what happened, and why it happened and discuss how you can avoid similar situations or limit the blast radius of similar incidents in the future. As always, these retrospective sessions should be completely blameless. The purpose is to find out why your processes allowed the service to get into a state where it required a human to fix it. You should then look to use this information to make changes in an attempt to improve your mean time to recovery (MTTR)—one of the core DORA metrics correlated with high-performing teams. If you look at these sessions instead as an excuse to find and place blame on individuals, then they won't be an effective use of your time and will just serve to damage the psychological safety of your team members.

If you do alert when no action is needed, you risk "alert fatigue." Alert fatigue occurs when there is too much noise coming from your alerting system. If developers and operations teams are bombarded with the same alerts constantly even when the system is fine, they will become desensitized to them and eventually most likely start to ignore them. If you ever hear your developers responding to an alert with something along the lines of "Oh, that alert is fine. It always goes off," then you're experiencing symptoms of alert fatigue.

Alert fatigue can happen when your alerts are poorly configured. Perhaps your alerts are configured too sensitively, for example, and trigger too often. If developers are called out often for false positives, their trust in the alerting system will be damaged.

Alert fatigue can also be caused by simply overwhelming development teams with too many alerts, particularly when many of them don't require immediate attention. This can happen because you've been simply overzealous with your alerting, you haven't cleared out or reconfigured alerts as the system has evolved, or you don't have a good way of prioritizing alerts that require attention now vs. "tickets" that can be addressed within working hours or in the upcoming days or weeks.

Thankfully, there are other ways to know if your system is in a good working state or not. Responding to alerts is (and should be) inherently reactive. Alerts will trigger your on-call process and wake developers up in the middle of the night. The last thing you want is sleepy, grumpy developers who no longer trust the alerting system. But there are other types of monitoring available. *Site Reliability Engineering* outlines three different types of monitoring output: "alerts," which signify something wrong with the system that requires immediate action; "tickets," which signify something wrong with the system that requires action in perhaps a few days but where no damage will come from having no immediate human input: and "logs," which are information recorded for diagnostic or debugging purposes but that no one is necessarily expected to look at unless prompted to.

There are ways to use your monitoring to be slightly more proactive, however. You might set up dashboards that display graphs of certain metrics you measure. You can display this on a screen in your workspace or go over them in standups. This can help spot patterns that might suggest issues in the future or proactively see that no issues are occurring that have been missed by alerts. You might also review your logs, again either in standups, ad hoc, or in dedicated sessions. You might look for new error logs in your application, or the highest grouping of similar error logs, and dig into why users might be being served these errors in specific scenarios.

Despite this, monitoring is inherently always going to be somewhat reactive. You can only create dashboards, logs, and metrics for error states you already know about. These known unknowns are important to keep an eye on, but in the industry these days—where your system might be distributed across tens of microservices across dozens of replicas in the cloud, perhaps in a Kubernetes cluster with a mesh system in place or a serverless lambda function in AWS with API Gateway sitting in front of it— the complexity of your system might lead to *unknown* unknowns, errors you may not even have thought of yet. In these cases monitoring your known error states might not help you. To cover *unknown* unknowns you need to work on the observability of your software applications.

Observability

As Charity Majors says in her book *Observability Engineering*: "Monitoring is for the known-unknowns, but observability is for the unknown-unknowns." This distinction highlights the critical difference between traditional monitoring approaches and the more holistic practice of observability.

Observability will allow you to understand the inner workings of your software application, including any system state your software can potentially get itself into, even if the software has never been in that particular state before and it wasn't something you would have predicted could happen. At its core, observability is the ability to understand the internal state of a system based on the outputs it produces. It's about gaining insight into what is happening inside your software without necessarily having predefined expectations of what might go wrong.

In other words, observability allows engineers to ask and answer open-ended questions about their systems, often revealing unexpected behaviors or issues. You should be able to answer questions like

- Which users or regions are experiencing the most issues, and what are the common factors?

- What experience has any specific user had today when going through our frontend journey?

- What does every user who is experiencing problems with our journey today have in common?

- Why are things slow for one specific user?

- What errors have occurred for any specific user on a particular day?

- Can you find the above even if you've never seen that error before?

If you can answer questions like this, then you have succeeded in implementing a good level of observability into your service. Having the data to do this involves quality telemetry data for traffic through your system, particularly data around three of the pillars of observability: logs, metrics, and traces. Logs provide a detailed, time-stamped record of discrete events that occurred in the system. Metrics offer quantitative data points that indicate the state of the system over time. Traces, on the other hand, provide a view of how requests or processes flow through various components of the system, enabling you to understand the relationships and dependencies within your software architecture.

The other important aspect of observability to remember is that observability is what Charity Majors describes in her book as a "sociotechnical concept." Just having the technical systems and the data in place doesn't mean you are practicing observability well. You need the cultural and organizational systems in place alongside them. It's not just about having the right tools in place to monitor and understand a system's behavior; it's also about how these tools are utilized by the people within an organization. The value of observability lies in its ability to provide insights that help teams collaborate more effectively, make informed decisions, and respond to incidents quickly. This is particularly important in environments that embrace practices like DevOps or Site Reliability Engineering (SRE), where shared responsibility for system health and continuous learning are key.

Observability, for example, requires learning from past incidents and adapting systems and processes accordingly. This learning process involves technical analysis but is also a social activity. Teams conduct postmortems, share knowledge, and adjust practices based on the insights gained from observable data. The effectiveness of this learning process depends on your organizational culture and how well the technical data is integrated into the social and organizational processes. That dependence is the reason observability is dubbed a "sociotechnical concept," rather than just a technical concept.

The effectiveness of observability really does depend heavily on how well it integrates with these processes. Observability tools might provide vast amounts of data, but it's the human interpretation, creativity, and collaboration that turn this data into actionable insights. You don't just "get" observability by buying an "observability tool" off the shelf, despite some of the marketing around these tools. Instead you get observability by implementing quality telemetry data through your software systems and allowing your development teams to learn from and investigate this data as a part of their cultural approach to software engineering.

Tools for Monitoring

There are a lot of practical tools on the market for assisting your team in their journey to better monitoring and observability. Some are open source, whereas others are paid solutions with enterprise support.

To help you on your journey toward a practical application of some of the concepts we've covered, it might be helpful to have a list of some of the more ubiquitous monitoring and observability tooling across the industry:

ELK Stack (Elasticsearch, Logstash, Kibana) is a collection of open source tools used for centralized logging and log analysis. Elasticsearch handles search and storage of log data, Logstash processes and ingests logs from various sources, and Kibana provides visualization through dashboards. ELK Stack is commonly used to collect, search, and analyze log data, offering a centralized view of logs from multiple systems. ELK is particularly useful for identifying patterns in logs, correlating events across distributed systems, and gaining insights into system performance from log data.

Jaeger is an open source distributed tracing tool designed to monitor and troubleshoot transactions across complex, microservices-based architectures. It allows tracing the flow of requests through different services, helping users to identify latency issues and errors within the system. Distributed tracing tools like Jaeger can be critical in understanding the interactions and performance across various services. By capturing traces that represent the flow of requests through different services, these tools can help teams identify latency bottlenecks, understand dependencies between services, and diagnose performance issues. They can help provide visibility into how individual requests are handled and where delays or errors might be occurring.

Prometheus is an open source monitoring and alerting toolkit focused on capturing and querying time-series data. It includes PromQL, a query language that allows users to create complex queries and generate alerts based on specific conditions. It integrates well with Grafana for visualization, offering a combination for real-time monitoring, alerting, and visualization in dashboards and graphs. Prometheus is fairly widely used, particularly in cloud-native environments, for monitoring application and infrastructure performance, particularly for time-series data.

Grafana is an open source platform for visualizing metrics and creating interactive dashboards. It integrates with multiple data sources, such as Prometheus, InfluxDB, and Elasticsearch, enabling users to build custom dashboards that display real-time data. Grafana is frequently employed for visualizing and exploring metrics, logs, and traces in cohesive dashboards and graphs.

Datadog is a cloud-based monitoring and analytics platform offering tools to monitor infrastructure, applications, logs, and user experience. It supports integration with a wide range of technologies and services, allowing for the collection and correlation of data across different parts of the technology stack. Datadog is commonly used to gain visibility into system performance in both cloud and on-premises environments. You can create alerts and dashboards, check logs, check request traces, and investigate metrics all within Datadog, making it something of a one-stop shop for monitoring across your software estate.

OpenTelemetry is an open source observability framework that provides a set of APIs, libraries, agents, and instrumentation to generate, collect, and export telemetry data, such as traces, metrics, and logs. It is designed to work with multiple observability backends, making it a vendor-neutral solution. OpenTelemetry is often adopted to standardize the way telemetry data is collected across distributed systems, enabling better integration and interoperability with various monitoring tools.

PagerDuty is a cloud-based incident management platform that helps teams respond to critical system issues in real time. It integrates with monitoring tools to trigger alerts based on predefined conditions and routes those alerts to the appropriate on-call personnel, including calling out to mobile phone numbers for those on call.

These tools and frameworks, and a huge list of others that aren't covered here, can each help play a part in providing the technical capabilities that address different aspects of system health, performance monitoring, and troubleshooting. You need to also make sure that your teams have the processes, culture, and accountability to use tooling like this effectively.

Accountability

Accountability in the context of production reliability refers to the obligation of individuals and teams to take responsibility for the systems they build, maintain, and operate. This means being answerable for both the successes and failures of those systems, as well as the ongoing commitment to improve them over time. When accountability is embedded within an organization's culture, it creates a sense of ownership that motivates teams to prioritize reliability in their work.

One of the primary ways accountability contributes to production reliability is by ensuring that every team member understands their role in the system's success. Engineers who are accountable for the stability and performance of their systems in production are more likely to know what it takes to write software fit for their users and the organization's needs. They are also more likely to adhere to best practices, follow proper processes, and take proactive steps to prevent issues before they occur.

For example, an engineer who knows they will be on the hook for any production incidents caused by their code is more likely to write thorough tests, conduct comprehensive code reviews, and ensure that their deployments are safe and well-planned. This sense of personal responsibility drives better decision-making and ultimately leads to more reliable systems.

Fostering a Culture of Accountability

Creating a culture of accountability requires intentional effort from leadership and a clear communication of expectations. Organizations must establish processes and policies that support accountability at every level, from individual contributors to teams and departments. Key strategies for fostering accountability to maintain production reliability might include

1. **Clear Roles and Responsibilities:** Accountability
    starts with clarity. Each team member should
    have a clear understanding of their roles and
    responsibilities regarding production systems. This
    includes knowing what they are responsible for,
    what they are expected to deliver, and how their
    work impacts the overall reliability of the system.
    When roles are well-defined, there is less ambiguity,
    and it becomes easier to hold individuals and teams
    accountable for their contributions.

2. **Ownership of Services:** A critical aspect of
    accountability is the concept of service ownership.
    Teams or individuals who develop a service should
    also be responsible for maintaining it in production.
    This end-to-end ownership ensures that the same
    people who build the system are also accountable
    for its performance, reliability, and uptime. When
    teams own their services, they are more invested in
    ensuring those services run smoothly and are more
    likely to address issues promptly.

3. **Blameless Postmortems:** Accountability should
    not be about assigning blame when things go
    wrong, but rather about understanding what
    happened and how to prevent it in the future.
    Blameless postmortems are a powerful tool for
    fostering accountability while promoting a culture
    of learning and continuous improvement. After an
    incident, teams should conduct a thorough review
    to understand the root causes, what actions led
    to the incident, and what can be done to prevent
    it from happening again. By focusing on learning

rather than blaming, teams are more likely to take ownership of issues and work collaboratively to improve system reliability.

4. **Metrics and Monitoring:** To maintain accountability, it is essential to measure and monitor key metrics related to production reliability. Metrics like uptime, performance against SLIs, performance against the error budget, mean time to recovery (MTTR), and incident frequency provide quantifiable data that teams can use to assess their performance. Regularly reviewing these metrics helps teams stay aware of their system's health and identify areas where improvements are needed. When teams are accountable for their metrics, they are more motivated to maintain high standards and work toward continuous improvement.

5. **On-Call Rotations:** On-call rotations are a practical way to distribute accountability across the team. When engineers know they will be responsible for responding to incidents during their on-call shift, they are more likely to design systems that are resilient and easier to troubleshoot. On-call rotations also ensure that knowledge and responsibility for production systems are shared across the team, preventing burnout and building a culture where everyone is accountable for reliability.

6. **Continuous Feedback Loops:** Accountability is reinforced through continuous feedback. Regular feedback sessions, retrospectives, and performance reviews provide opportunities to recognize

achievements, address challenges, and set goals for improvement. When teams receive feedback on their contributions to system reliability, they are more likely to stay engaged and committed to maintaining high standards.

The Impact of Accountability on System Reliability

When accountability is deeply ingrained in an organization's culture, it has a profound impact on system reliability. Engineers who feel accountable for their work are more likely to

- **Prioritize Reliability:** Accountability motivates teams to prioritize reliability in their work. This means considering the potential impact of changes on production, thoroughly testing new features, and being cautious with deployments. Engineers are more likely to think critically about how their actions will affect the system's stability and take proactive steps to mitigate risks.

- **Proactively Address Issues:** Accountable teams do not wait for problems to escalate. They actively monitor their systems, respond quickly to incidents, and implement long-term fixes to prevent future occurrences. This proactive approach reduces downtime and ensures that issues are resolved before they can significantly impact users.

- **Collaborate Effectively:** Accountability encourages collaboration across teams. When everyone is responsible for the reliability of the system, silos break down, and teams work together to address challenges. This collaborative effort leads to faster incident resolution, better knowledge sharing, and more robust systems.

- **Drive Continuous Improvement:** Accountability drives a culture of continuous improvement. Teams regularly review their performance, identify areas for improvement, and implement changes that enhance system reliability. This iterative approach ensures that reliability is not a one-time goal but an ongoing commitment.

- **Enhance Customer Trust:** Reliable systems build customer trust, and accountability is key to maintaining that trust. When customers know that a company is committed to providing reliable services, they are more likely to stay loyal and recommend the service to others. Accountability ensures that reliability remains a top priority, leading to long-term customer satisfaction.

Challenges and Considerations

While accountability is essential for maintaining production reliability, it is not without challenges. Organizations must be mindful of potential pitfalls, such as

- **Avoiding a Culture of Fear:** It is crucial to distinguish between accountability and blame. Accountability should not create a culture of fear where individuals are afraid to make mistakes. Instead, it should promote ownership and learning. Leaders must ensure that accountability is framed positively, focusing on growth and improvement rather than punishment.

- **Balancing Accountability with Support:** Teams need the right tools, resources, and support to fulfil their accountability. Organizations should provide access to monitoring tools, incident management systems, and training to help teams succeed. Without adequate support, holding teams accountable can lead to frustration and burnout.

- **Ensuring Fairness:** Accountability should be distributed fairly across the team. No single individual should bear the brunt of responsibility for the entire system. On-call rotations, shared ownership, and clear communication help distribute accountability and prevent any one person from becoming overwhelmed.

Accountability is a powerful driver of production reliability. By fostering a culture where individuals and teams take ownership of their systems, organizations can ensure that reliability is prioritized, issues are addressed proactively, and continuous improvement is embraced. When accountability is embedded in the organization's DNA, it leads to more reliable systems, satisfied customers, and a stronger competitive position in the market.

Ultimately, accountability is not just about holding people responsible—it is about empowering teams to take pride in their work, collaborate effectively, and strive for excellence.

Key Takeaways

- **CI/CD Pipelines Streamline Workflows:** Automating integration, testing, and deployment through CI/CD pipelines reduces manual errors, ensures consistency, and accelerates software delivery. However, it's essential to balance speed with software quality, reliability, and comprehensive testing.

- **Testing Is Crucial at Every Stage:** CI/CD testing is not limited to the final stages of development; it must be built into every step of the pipeline, including unit tests, integration tests, and end-to-end tests. This ensures that all changes are vetted before production.

- **Automation Enhances Reliability:** Automation in build processes, testing, deployment, and monitoring minimizes manual intervention and errors, ensuring consistency and faster deployments. Reliable automation helps maintain high-quality releases even at a faster pace.

- **Balancing Speed and Reliability:** Although CI/CD can accelerate deployment, prioritizing software reliability remains vital. Strategies like error budgets, service-level indicators (SLIs), and service-level objectives (SLOs) can help maintain this balance.

- **Monitoring and Observability:** Effective monitoring is essential for maintaining reliability and ensuring that the speed of deployments doesn't compromise quality. Observability adds a proactive layer by offering deeper insights into system behavior.

- **Accountability and Culture:** Successful implementation of CI/CD depends on fostering a culture of accountability, where teams take ownership of the services they develop and maintain in production. Blameless postmortems and continuous feedback loops are crucial for learning from failures and improving reliability.

The next chapter will cover current trends in CI/CD and what the future might hold for CI/CD against the backdrop of the ever-changing world of software engineering.

CHAPTER 5

The Future of CI/CD

While CI/CD may have started as a niche subject among a group of forward-thinking software professionals, it is now in common use across the industry. 68.6% of software developers polled as part of the 2024 Stack Overflow survey[1] now say that practicing CI/CD is at least something that is available to them at the organization they work for.

So what next for CI/CD? How can we continue to make progress in this area to ensure that we are continuing to improve our ways of working and progressing toward being able to meet the goals of our organizations more efficiently and more effectively? Let's talk about some of the current and potential future trends for CI/CD.

DevOps to NoOps …

In 2008, an IT consultant named Patrick Debois recognized that the way development teams and Ops teams were working together wasn't optimal and decided this needed to change. In October 2009, he held the very first DevOpsDays conference in Ghent, Belgium, which he billed as "The conference that brings development and operations together." Around the same time, in 2009, John Allspaw and Paul Hammond delivered a talk at the 2009 Velocity conference entitled "10+ Deploys per Day—Dev and Ops Cooperation at Flickr," and the idea of DevOps started to take hold in the industry.

---

[1] https://survey.stackoverflow.co/2024/professional-developers/

© Tommy Clark 2025
T. Clark, *CI/CD Unleashed*, Apress Pocket Guides,
https://doi.org/10.1007/979-8-8688-1209-5_5

In 2016, Google's site reliability team released their book *Site Reliability Engineering* (they described in the book that their processes could be viewed as an implementation of DevOps), which again shifted the way that development teams thought about maintaining their production services.

There have been countless practices following the "-ops"-suffixed nomenclature since the rise of DevOps in 2009, equally trying to change the way that development teams operate—with varying levels of success. DevSecOps describes the act of integrating security into every step of your software delivery lifecycle. ChatOps involves integrating DevOps workflows and tools into chat platforms like Slack or Microsoft Teams, enabling to manage systems directly from their chat environment. GitOps applies DevOps principles using Git as a single source of truth for infrastructure and application code, allowing for automated deployments and rollbacks, while NoOps aims to eliminate the need for a dedicated operations team by automating all aspects of infrastructure management, allowing developers to focus entirely on coding and deploying applications.

The fact of the matter of course is that the right approach to take in order to deliver software will be specific to your business, but there are some trends that have caught on since 2009 that might aid your development team in implementing good CI/CD practices.

Cloud-Managed Services

For years, organizations have relied on manually provisioned and maintained systems in the cloud to handle their computing needs. These systems, while efficient, required maintenance, oversight, and resources. Managing servers, ensuring uptime, and scaling resources to meet demand often meant that organizations had to devote substantial time and energy to managing their cloud infrastructure in GCP or AWS. This was not only costly but also diverted focus from core business objectives.

However, the advent of cloud-managed services has revolutionized how development and operations teams host their software services. Cloud-managed services (e.g., in AWS, the likes of S3, SES, SNS, SQS, EKS, RDS, DynamoDB, among others) provide ready-to-use, fully managed solutions that eliminate the need for manual intervention in infrastructure management. These services are designed to be scalable, resilient, reliable, and cost-effective without much operations input, allowing businesses to focus on what they do best—innovating and delivering value to their customers without worrying about the underlying infrastructure.

One of the significant advantages of cloud-managed services is their scalability. Take Amazon S3 (Simple Storage Service), for example. It offers virtually unlimited storage that can grow seamlessly with your data needs. Instead of investing in physical storage hardware and managing its capacity, businesses can rely on S3 to automatically scale, ensuring that storage is never a bottleneck. Similarly, services like SQS (Simple Queue Service) allow organizations to decouple and distribute workloads efficiently, ensuring that their applications can handle spikes in demand without requiring manual intervention to scale resources.

These cloud-managed services can also improve overall efficiency and reliability. Cloud-managed AWS services like SQS, RDS, S3, etc. are designed to integrate seamlessly with other AWS offerings, creating a cohesive environment where different services interact effortlessly. This capability allows organizations to build complex workflows with minimal effort, leveraging the AWS ecosystem (or, indeed, whichever cloud provider you are using). The big cloud providers, like Amazon and Google, also operate data centers all around the world, providing robust redundancy and failover capabilities that are built into their managed services by default, providing the kind of business continuity and reliability it would be difficult for a software development team to implement and maintain manually on their own.

You can also significantly reduce operational overhead this way. With services like SES (Simple Email Service) and SNS (Simple Notification Service), businesses can automate their communication processes, like sending emails or push notifications, without needing to maintain their own messaging infrastructure to do so. This not only reduces complexity but also ensures better ongoing security and reliability, as cloud providers will be managing and continuously improving these services behind the scenes without your team having to worry or bother themselves with the details.

Security is another critical area where cloud-managed services can excel. By leveraging services like AWS Identity and Access Management (IAM) or Google Cloud's Security Command Center, your team can implement robust security policies with minimal effort. You can get built-in encryption, access controls, and monitoring tools without the need to develop and maintain these capabilities in-house.

The future of cloud-managed services is poised for even greater advancements, as organizations increasingly rely on cloud solutions to power their operations. The focus is shifting from basic infrastructure management to more sophisticated uses of cloud capabilities. We have already seen and can anticipate further developments in AI and machine learning, with cloud providers like AWS and GCP continuing to expand their tools and services, enabling organizations to harness their datass full potential.

Hybrid and multi-cloud strategies are also becoming more prevalent as organizations recognize the value of diversifying their cloud investments across multiple providers and avoid being locked into one cloud provider, in order to reduce risk and optimize costs. Cloud providers are already responding to this trend by offering tools that facilitate seamless integration with other vendors, ensuring businesses can maintain some flexibility and avoid vendor lock-in.

All of this makes software delivery and the reliability of production easier for development teams to manage, ultimately improving their deployment processes and making continuous deployment hopefully a more attractive proposition.

Serverless

With the advent of cloud and cloud-managed services, not many teams are still running their applications directly on their own physical servers. And most might argue that it was too much work and effort and distracted teams from their core goal of delivering features for customers. They'd point to having to be responsible for everything from setting up physical servers, installing and configuring the operating system, as well as the physical space that's required. They'd talk perhaps about the difficulty of ensuring high availability, scaling the services, performing regular maintenance, and handling failures.

Many might say the same now too, about managing a Kubernetes cluster. Kubernetes is an incredibly powerful orchestration framework allowing for automated deployment and scaling of containerized applications. But this power comes with a lot of complexity. Setting up a Kubernetes cluster requires in-depth knowledge of its architecture, including understanding components like pods, services, deployments, mesh networks, and ingress controllers. Even once the cluster is operational, managing the lifecycle of applications, handling updates, monitoring performance, and ensuring security and fault tolerance all require continuous attention and expertise. Developers and operations teams have to handle the intricacies of networking, storage, and configuration management within the cluster by themselves.

Serverless computing, on the other hand, offers a refreshing departure for development teams, from all of these complexities. Instead of managing servers, infrastructure, and scaling concerns, development teams can now focus on writing code. The cloud provider can take care of the rest—automatically provisioning the necessary resources, scaling applications in response to demand, and handling much of the operational overhead. Code can be deployed to, for example, an AWS lambda function in the cloud and sit there ready to be executed without the team concerning themselves with servers or clusters. This simplicity is a game-changer, as it frees up teams to concentrate solely on their business logic and actual code.

In a serverless environment, there is no need to provision or maintain servers, manage runtimes, or even think about scaling; everything is handled automatically by the cloud provider. The focus shifts entirely to developing the application, allowing for a much more streamlined and agile workflow. The operational burdens—like capacity planning, patching, and scaling—are abstracted away, enabling teams to deploy and iterate on new features faster.

The pay-as-you-go pricing model typical of serverless platforms is another draw for development teams, making sure that organizations only pay for capacity that they actually use and scaling to zero during quiet periods, further optimizing costs and eliminating waste and redundancy. This allows organizations to reduce costs, increase agility, and accelerate time to market for new features and applications. It also has the benefit of democratizing access to powerful computing resources, making it easier for those in smaller teams and startups to innovate and compete with bigger, more resource-heavy enterprises.

This abstraction away from some of the complexities of infrastructure management can allow teams to focus on what truly matters—delivering value to their customers—without getting bogged down by the operational challenges that come with managing servers or Kubernetes clusters.

Serverless Pipelines

As was mentioned above, serverless computing has revolutionized the way we think about infrastructure, and its impact on our CI/CD pipelines and processes is no exception. By adopting serverless principles, organizations can streamline not just their production infrastructure but also the infrastructure required to keep their CI/CD processes running, reducing complexity and focusing on delivering high-quality software through their pipelines more efficiently.

One example of the trend toward less maintenance-heavy infrastructure here is the move away from self-hosted CI/CD tools like Jenkins or TeamCity. Jenkins in particular was long considered the de facto king of CI/CD tooling, but its dominance has been very much challenged in recent times by more modern, cloud-native tooling like GitHub Actions, GitLab CI/CD, AWS CodePipeline, or Google Cloud Build.

The Continuous Delivery Foundation's annual *State of CI/CD Report* shows how rapid this decline has been, with 32% of practitioners surveyed using self-hosted CI/CD tools like Jenkins or TeamCity in Q1 2022, compared with just 17% two years later in Q1 of 2024.

The reason for this decline is simple. Jenkins, while powerful, requires considerable maintenance and infrastructure management. You need to ensure that your Jenkins server is available, properly configured, and scalable enough to handle multiple concurrent builds across your entire organization. It requires management of plugins, manual upgrades, monitoring of disk and CPU usage, and security and access management. This can be a particularly resource-heavy exercise for an operations or development team. These challenges can detract from the actual core goal of CI/CD—continuous and reliable integration and delivery of code.

In contrast, CI/CD can be very straightforward if, for example, your source code repositories are stored in GitHub. The vast majority of professional developers use GitHub as a place to store code,[2] and it's used by the world's largest organizations, from Google to Netflix, to Microsoft, to Facebook. For those GitHub repositories, you can get started with a CI/CD pipeline by simply placing a .yaml file into a specific directory in your repository (namely, `.github/workflows`). You don't need to provision infrastructure or consider scaling or the maintenance of virtual servers. All you need to do is add config files to your repository, and the rest is handled for you.

---

[2] 82.8% of them according to the 2020 Stack Overflow Developer Survey. `https://survey.stackoverflow.co/2020`

Infrastructure as Code in Code, Rather Than Config

The rise of infrastructure as code (IaC) has been one of the most transformative trends in software development in recent years. Initially, IaC was embraced through configuration files and domain-specific languages (DSLs), with tools like Helm charts for Kubernetes and Terraform for cloud infrastructure management leading the charge.

One of the primary challenges of tools like these was the rigidity of DSLs and configuration files. These tools, by design, are limited in their expressiveness compared with full-fledged programming languages. And as infrastructure needs grew more complex, this limitation has become more and more apparent.

For example, configuration files like YAML or JSON are not inherently flexible or capable of handling complex logic. While it's possible to use templating engines to introduce some level of dynamism, the resulting code often becomes unwieldy and difficult to maintain. Debugging and testing these configurations is also difficult, particularly compared with debugging traditional code, which has led to a steeper learning curve and more potential for errors in untested infrastructure configuration files.

The separation between application code and infrastructure configuration also helped create a siloed approach to development. Developers had to switch contexts between writing application code and managing infrastructure configuration, which could lead to inconsistencies and slower development cycles. Some developers have a much lower comfort level with tools like Terraform, Ansible, or Helm, and it led to infrastructure teams who spend their time working on configuring infrastructure files and separate development teams who work on features before throwing their code over to the former to manage it in production. The need for a more integrated approach became increasingly apparent as the complexity and scale of modern applications and cloud infrastructure has grown.

There is an alternative though, and some organizations are shifting from configuration-based IaC to code-centric IaC, exemplified by platforms like Pulumi and AWS Cloud Development Kit (CDK). Tools like Pulumi and CDK allow developers to define the infrastructure their software sits on using the same general-purpose programming languages they're used to writing for feature development—TypeScript, Python, Java, C#, etc.

Unlike configuration files, programming languages provide robust features such as loops, conditionals, functions, and error handling, which allows for far more dynamic and sophisticated infrastructure definitions. For instance, instead of relying on templating or complex configuration files, which can be pulled in by other declarative configuration files, a developer can use familiar constructs like loops and conditionals directly in their IaC code, which not only simplifies the code but can also help make it more readable and maintainable.

With this code-centric IaC, developers can also write unit tests and integration tests and even use mocking frameworks to simulate cloud resources. We've already spoken about how important automated testing is and how it can improve confidence in code going straight to production. When things do go wrong, development teams can debug their infrastructure code just as they typically would debug their software.

These tools also provide a lower barrier to entry for developers to manage their infrastructure. With continuous deployment, it is important that a development team feels accountable for their code in production and that they feel comfortable with their production infrastructure. These tools allow for that by allowing for the use of the same programming language for both application code and infrastructure code, which reduces context switching and allows for better integration between application logic and infrastructure provisioning.

For example, in a serverless application, the boundaries between code and infrastructure can be really blurred. With tools like AWS CDK, the development team can define serverless resources such as Lambda functions, API Gateways, and DynamoDB tables using the same language they use for the application logic. This all helps create a more cohesive development experience, enabling faster iteration, more consistent deployments, and a development team that is comfortable and feels accountable for their production infrastructure and the code that runs on it.

AI and Its Use in CI/CD

We would be remiss to discuss the future of the software industry without mentioning artificial intelligence. Since the introduction of ChatGPT to the public in 2022, the landscape and perception of technology has been fundamentally transformed. According to the 2024 *Global Software Buying Trends Report* by Gartner, 92% of business are considering buying AI-powered software, while according to Stack Overflow's 2024 *Developer Survey*, 76% of developers are either using AI in their daily development process or plan to start doing so this year. Deloitte's 2002 *State of AI* report found that 94% of business leaders believe AI will be critical to the success of their business over the next five years.

This recent boom and widespread adoption of AI is not just reshaping the software industry; it's revolutionizing entire sectors, from finance to healthcare, by enabling smarter decision-making, personalized user experiences, and more efficient operations. As AI continues to advance, its role in software development is expected to grow even more critical. This will be felt across the whole industry and not least in CI/CD where it is likely we'll continue to see innovation.

There are some tools already that are helping drive this AI-assisted innovation in continuous integration.

Examples of AI Tooling for CI/CD

- **Test.ai:** Test.ai automates the generation and execution of functional tests using AI. This can help improve coverage and free the QA team up to look at more complex testing scenarios.

- **Magalix:** Magalix uses machine learning to automatically adapt application and resource usage accordingly. This helps reduce overspending and redundant resourcing and dynamically scales your infrastructure as per your needs.

- **Diffblue Cover:** Diffblue Cover uses AI to automatically generate unit tests for Java code, aiming to improve code coverage and save development time.

- **Qwiet AI:** Qwiet AI is a tool that scans your codebase and uses AI to discover, prioritize, and generate automatic fixes for security vulnerabilities that might exist in your code.

- **DeepCode AI:** As above, DeepCode AI is a static application security testing (SAST) tool that uses static analysis to uncover and automatically fix security vulnerabilities in your codebase. It is built into the popular static analysis tool Snyk.

- **Mabl:** A test automation platform that uses AI to generate tests and extend test coverage.

- **GitLab Auto DevOps:** GitLab's Auto DevOps feature uses AI to automatically detect the type of project and apply CI/CD best practices, including automated testing, security scans, and deployment strategies.

These are just a number of tools that allow you to utilize AI somewhere in your CI/CD pipeline to add reliability, quality, or security. As AI continues to evolve, the possibilities for enhancing your development process and deployment pipelines will only expand, promising even more innovative solutions in the near future.

A Friendly Warning

Artificial Intelligence has become an increasingly powerful tool in software development, offering a range of efficiencies that can significantly accelerate your software delivery. AI-driven tools can automate repetitive tasks, optimize your algorithms, and even generate code snippets for your developers to plunder, allowing developers to focus on the more complex and creative aspects of programming. These benefits can lead to faster development cycles, reduced costs, and even improved quality if used carefully.

But there are risks to look out for when introducing AI into your software delivery processes. While AI can generate code quickly, it may not fully understand the context or nuanced requirements of a particular project and could lead to bugs or vulnerabilities that might be overlooked by human developers. These issues could result in the introduction of security or functionality flaws into your CI/CD processes that are difficult to detect until they cause significant damage.

There's also a trend whereby developers and QA engineers might use LLMs to write their unit tests for them. AI-generated tests, though, might easily miss important context or business logic specific to your application. Unit tests need to be closely aligned with the intended functionality of the code they are testing. An LLM, despite its capabilities, may lack the nuanced understanding of the specific business requirements and the rationale behind certain code decisions, leading to tests that might pass without truly validating the desired behavior of the software.

TDD, in contrast, ensures that the development process is tightly aligned with the requirements of your software. It fosters a deeper understanding of the problem domain, by forcing developers to clearly articulate the expected behavior of the software in the form of tests before any implementation begins, that is, because tests are written based on the expected behavior of the code, developers are compelled to think carefully about the design and functionality and any potential missed requirements, before writing any implementation code. This leads to more deliberate and thoughtful code that directly addresses the software's intended requirements without bloat.

With its focus on writing just enough code to pass the tests, TDD also encourages developers to write simpler, more focused code. This often results in a cleaner codebase, as developers avoid over-engineering or adding unnecessary features that are not explicitly tested.

This all results in high-quality tests with good coverage of the business requirements, which can be used as documentation on what the code is *supposed to do*. AI-generated tests will not provide you with any of these benefits, instead just providing you with good code coverage. AI-generated code is better used in your application code, rather than in the automated test code that acts as your final quality gate for serving your code to production users.

Conclusion

As we reach the end of this exploration into continuous integration and continuous deployment, it's essential to reflect on the core message of this book: CI/CD is as much about people as it is about technology. While the tools and processes that enable these ways of working are of course critical, CI/CD is ultimately about collaborating better.

Integrating your code into the rest of your team's code multiple times a day and deploying the resulting build to real production users every time requires automated testing, a sensible deployment strategy, accountability, small and sensibly sliced tickets, and a reliable and repeatable pipeline, but it also requires your developers to talk to each other and work together.

Throughout this book, we've discussed how CI/CD practices help in managing the inherent risks of software development, allowing teams to deliver high-quality software rapidly and reliably and delivering to the market before competitors. We've talked about the data-driven insights around frequent deployments. We saw that deploying frequently and having developers who are comfortable in production not only improves the reliability of your software but also means you're more likely to achieve your organizational goals. These practices are not just about automation or pipelines; they're about people, organizational culture, and risk.

With the recent AI boom and the inevitable changes in software development, a lot is going to change, but software development will always be about people, risk, and delivering working software for users. Those things will stay constant.

No matter what new technologies or methodologies emerge, the principles of CI/CD—a focus on reducing the risk of deployments, increasing collaboration, and continuously delivering value in a safe way—will remain crucial.

As you move forward in your journey with CI/CD, I hope you've gained a deeper understanding of how these practices can transform not just your software delivery processes but also the way your team works together. Remember, delivering software is about people. Embrace the collaborative nature of CI/CD, and you'll be well-equipped to handle whatever the future of software development holds.

Index

© Tommy Clark 2025
T. Clark, *CI/CD Unleashed*, Apress Pocket Guides,
https://doi.org/10.1007/979-8-8688-1209-5

R

Reducing toil, 116, 117
Risk management, 35
Rolling deployments, 48–51, 105
Rotation system, 65

S

SAST, *see* Static application security testing (SAST)
Serverless, 139, 140
   pipelines, 140, 141
Service-level agreements (SLAs), 28, 98, 110, 111
Service-level indicator (SLI), 109
Service-level objectives (SLOs), 28, 110, 111, 117
Service ownership, 127
SES, *see* Simple Email Service (SES)
Simple Email Service (SES), 138
Site reliability engineering (SRE), 80
   automation, 116, 117
   DevOps, 113
   DevOps and, 117, 118
   engineering-first mindset, 115, 116
   time allocation, 114, 115
   velocity and safety, 113, 114
Skcepticism, 12
SLAs, *see* Service-level agreements (SLAs)
SLI, *see* Service-level indicator (SLI)

SLOs, *see* Service-level objectives (SLOs)
Small releases, 32–36
Smoke testing, 106, 107
Simple Notification Service (SNS), 138
SNS, *see* Simple Notification Service (SNS)
SonarQube, 28
Source control, 54, 55
SRE, *see* Site reliability engineering (SRE)
Stakeholders notification, 107
Static application security testing (SAST), 145
Synchronous pull requests, 76
System reliability, 129, 130

T

TDD, *see* Test-driven development (TDD)
Terraform, 54
Test.ai, 145
Test-driven development (TDD), 21–24, 60
Testing
   automated, 28–30
   automated test suite, 21
   codebase, 20, 27, 28
   consistency, 22
   core functionality, 21
   legacy codebases, 20